Sociology for Nursing and Health Care

MARTIN JOSEPH

Polity Press

The right of Martin Joseph to be identified as author of this work has been asserted in accordance with the Copyright, Designs and Patents Act 1988.

First published in 1994 by Polity Press in association with Blackwell Publishers Ltd

Reprinted 1995

Editorial office:
Polity Press
65 Bridge Street
Cambridge CB2 1UR, UK

Marketing and production:
Blackwell Publishers Ltd
108 Cowley Road
Oxford OX4 1JF, UK

Blackwell Publishers Inc.
238 Main Street
Cambridge, MA 02142, USA

ISBN 0 7456 0905 8
ISBN 0 7456 0906 6 (pbk)

A CIP catalogue record for this book is available from the British Library

Library of Congress Cataloging in Publication Data
Joseph, Martin
  Sociology for nursing and health care / Martin Joseph.
    p. cm.
  Includes bibliographical references and index.
  ISBN 0–7456–0905–8 (acid-free paper). — ISBN 0–7456–0906–6 (pbk. acid-free paper)
  1. Nursing – Social aspects. 2. Social medicine. I. Title.
RT86.5.M36 1993
306.4'61-dc20   93–6879
                                                                                    CIP

Typeset in 10½ on 12 pt Plantin
by Photo·graphics, Honiton, Devon
Printed in Great Britain by Hartnolls Ltd, Bodmin, Cornwall

This book is printed on acid-free paper

For Maureen and Simon, Jonathan and Sarah

Contents

Detailed Chapter Contents

Foreword

This book is designed for beginning students on nursing courses but it could be useful for other courses in health care. The aims of the book are to explain what sociology is and especially to show how it can help the nurse in actual ward situations. One way to achieve this is through the use of extracts from books, journals, newspapers and case studies. The book contains many such extracts, which are derived from a number of sources, and it is hoped that teachers will find these helpful in preparing course work. For example, at the end of chapter 2 there are three case studies on ways of consulting patients, ward management, and other related issues. Such studies could be used not only for essay course work but also seminar presentations, debates, and so on.

A large group of students could, for instance, be broken down into sub-groups of three. Within each sub-group there would be a chairperson who would summarize the views of the group members and present a report to a plenary session when called upon to do so. The post of chairperson would, of course, be rotated. Proceeding in this way, the whole group should have the opportunity to hear the views of others, submit their own ideas and perhaps gain some public speaking and communication skills.

Another means of group learning is project works using the college library, say, as a resource centre.

Overall the book could be seen as an exercise in practical active critical sociology.

Having emphasized its aim in assisting sociology tutors, I hope the

book will also be helpful and interesting to nurses, student nurses
and general readers.

Acknowledgements

I should like to acknowledge the help I have received from friends and colleagues at Oxford Brookes University, the former Oxford Polytechnic. In particular, I must thank Peter George and Lesley Golding for their practical advice. I must especially acknowledge the constant support and wise suggestions I have received from Frank Webster throughout this period. I am grateful for all the help I have received from the university and the library, including the subject librarian Sian King, and from Jayne Plant and Christine Robson.

Finally, I must thank the staff of Polity Press, including David Held, Gill Motley and Debbie Seymour, for their enthusiasm and hard work. The mistakes are, of course, my own.

I dedicate the book to my family for their forbearance.

Martin Joseph
Oxford Brookes University

For permission to reprint copyright material the publishers gratefully acknowledge the following: Blackwell Publishers for extract from 'Health, Health Risks and Inequalities' by M. Calman and B. Johnson in *Journal of Sociology of Health & Illness*, Vol. 17 (1985) (Blackwell, 1985); and for table from *Sociology for Everyone* by Martin Joseph (Polity Press, 1990); Blackwell Publishers and Anne Oakley for table from *Women Confined* by Anne Oakley (Martin Robertson & Co. Ltd, 1980); Marion Boyars Publishers Ltd, London and New York, for

extract from *Disabling Professions* by I. Illich (Boyars, 1977); But-
terworth-Heinemann Limited for extract from *The Politics of Nursing*
by Jane Salvage (Heinemann Medical Books, 1985), Copyright ©
Jane Salvage 1985; The Central Statistical Office for two tables from
Social Trends (1991), table from *Social Trends* (1992), and table from
Inland Revenue & Social Trends (1991), Crown copyright; The Control-
ler of Her Majesty's Stationery Office for table from *New Earnings
Survey* (1984 & 1991), and two tables from *Health Trends* (1987 &
1990), Crown copyright; Curtis Brown Ltd., London, on behalf of
The Estate of Brian Inglis, for extract from *The Diseases of Civilisation*
by Brian Inglis (Hodder & Stoughton, 1981), Copyright © Brian
Inglis, 1981; Gower Publishing Company Limited for tables from
British Social Attitudes, The 5th Report, edited by R. Jowell, S. Witherspoon, L. Brook (Gower, 1988); Guardian News Service Ltd for
adaptation from 'The abuse of power in a rotten culture' by Melanie
Phillips, © *The Guardian*, in the *Guardian*, 7 August 1982, adaptation
from 'Stress blamed for teachers' health problems' by Paul Hoyland,
© *The Guardian*, in *The Guardian*, 17 November 1990, and adaptation
from 'Jammed machine gave woman 4,000 volt shock' by a Correspondent, © *The Guardian*, in the *Guardian*, 22 September 1990, and for
'Doctors "fail to respect nurses"' by C. Myhill, © *The Guardian*, in
the *Guardian*, 11 March 1991; HarperCollins Publishers Ltd for five
tables from *Social Class Differences in Britain* (Third Edition) by Ivan
Reid (Fontana, 1989); Hodder & Stoughton Publishers for extracts
from *Building and Using a Model of Nursing* by S. G. Wright (Edward
Arnold Publishers, 1986); The Macmillan Press Limited for extracts
from *Nursing in Conflict* by P. Owens and R. Glennerster (Macmillan,
1990); Ewan MacNaughton Associates, Syndication Agents for *The
Telegraph* plc, for 'Old people in homes face increasing fees burden'
by David Fletcher © *The Telegraph* plc, 1991, in the *Daily Telegraph*,
4 April 1991; and 'Breathing aid plea to save lung patients' by the
Health Service Correspondent, © *The Telegraph* plc, 1981, in the
Daily Telegraph, 3 April 1981; Newspaper Publishing plc for extract
from article by Jack O'Sullivan first published in *The Independent*,
22 March 1991; The Observer Ltd for 'Damning Report on Health
of Aborigines' by Dr N. Thomson, © Copyright *The Observer*, London, 17 February 1991, in *The Observer* newspaper, 17 February
1991; Penguin Books Ltd for extract from 'What is To be Done
About Illness and Health' by Jeannette Mitchell (Penguin Books,
1984), Copyright © The Socialist Society 1984; and for five tables
from *Inequalities in Health: The Health Divide*, by Margaret Whitehead

(Penguin Books, 1988) Copyright © Margaret Whitehead 1988; The Peters, Fraser & Dunlop Group Ltd for extract from 'Schools for Scandal' by John Collee in *The Observer Magazine*, 16 August 1992; Policy Journals Ltd for extract by R. Maxwell from *Reshaping the National Health Service*, edited by R. Maxwell, (Policy Journals, 1988); Random House UK Limited and the Estate of Brendan Behan for extract from *Borstal Boy* by Brendan Behan, (Hutchinson, 1964); Routledge (International Thomson Publishing Services Ltd) for extract from *Samples from English Culture* by J. Klein (Routledge & Kegan Paul, 1964); and extract from *Family and Kinship in East London* by M. Young and Willmot (Routledge & Kegan Paul, 1957); Routledge/Tavistock for extract and two tables from *Health and Lifestyles* by M. Blaxter (Tavistock/Routledge, 1990); Sage Publications Ltd for extract from *Medical Power and Social Knowledge* by B. S. Turner (Sage, 1987).

Polity Press apologize for any errors or omissions in the above list and would be grateful to be notified of any corrections that should be incorporated in any future edition or reprint of this volume.

1 An Introduction to Sociology

1 Aims of Sociology

What is sociology? Is it of any practical use? How can it help me in my work as a nurse? Will it aid my understanding of what is going on all around me? These are the sorts of basic questions you may ask. What are the answers?

First, try to put aside any prejudices you may have – that sociology is just common sense, that it complicates what is basically simple and obvious, and so on.

Secondly, try to make the subject helpful and personal to you, for example by working through the questions and case studies at the end of each chapter.

Sociology seeks to show how society (or the group) influences the individual. Most of us would like to see ourselves as free individuals – free to choose where we live, free to choose our mate, our friends and our lifestyle (the way we live generally). Sociology does not deny we have freedom of choice but it also shows we are less free than we think. We tend to associate with people from a similar background: thus nurses will tend to associate with colleagues after work; professional people will associate with other professionals, and so on. In this way we come to have the same beliefs as those we are close to: it is rather like the adage 'Birds of a feather flock together'.

Sociologists also show that we learn our *role* (or place) in society from our parents and later from teachers, friends and colleagues at work. For example, a young girl may copy her mother's behaviour in learning her future role as a woman. This is known as *socialization*: the process of learning our role. Later this woman may learn other roles. Thus if she attends nursing school she learns the role of nurse, in particular carrying out the correct procedures so that they become second nature. In this way she has been socialized to her role as a nurse.

Socialization is based on the assumption that human beings are learning 'animals', and that we learn the roles we are to play throughout our lives. There are several roles we could learn – for example, those of boy, girl, man, woman, doctor, father, mother, immigrant, grandparent, church elder, patient, nurse. This contrasts with the biological view that we inherit our behaviour from our genes.

Primary socialization is the term given to the earliest and most important socialization in a child's first years of life. Secondary socialization occurs later and is usually less deep; for example, occupational socialization as a nurse. Another example would be the immigrant who has to learn a new role in his or her new country.

2   The Views of Four Leading Sociologists

In answering the question 'What is sociology?' it may be helpful to consider the work of four leading sociologists, Peter Berger, Robert Merton, C. Wright Mills and Peter Worsley.

Peter Berger: the unofficial view

In his book *Invitation to Sociology* Peter Berger contends that the sociologist should always be questioning everything going on around (Berger 1966). This scepticism leads the sociologist to contrast what appears to be going on with what is *really* going on. The sociologist should have a strong desire to see what is happening behind the screens and to ask such questions as: is this family happy or is it a kind of prison for its members?

Thus sociologists should try to describe the varying viewpoints of all participants in a situation; for example, in describing a hospital a sociologist may present it from the viewpoint of the administrator, the consultant, doctors, nurses, paramedics, porters, kitchen staff, and so on. In doing this sociologists often give the unofficial view of what is going on rather than the official one, for instance by reflecting the viewpoint of the porter or the patient rather than that of the manager or the consultant.

It is this tendency to take seriously the unofficial view of what is going on, to question authority, that can make sociology unpopular with people in power. Yet this constant questioning of authority is part of the sociological task. It is not its aim to be popular. In fact, if all 'the good and the great' in the land were saying how useful sociology was, this would be a fair indication that it was not doing its job properly.

Robert Merton: manifest and latent functions

Robert Merton (1968) distinguishes between manifest and latent functions. The former are deliberate functions (of a hospital, school, etc.); the latter are the unintended consequences. Table 1.1 gives a few examples which illustrate this distinction. As already stated, the sociologist must distinguish between the real and the apparent; between facts and *ideologies* (see Glossary).

C. Wright Mills: private troubles and public issues

C. Wright Mills (1970) sees the task of the sociologist as being to develop what he calls the sociological imagination, which will enable its possessor to understand the hidden meaning of everyday life. In some ways Mills's approach is similar to Berger's, but Mills's special contribution to sociology is to provide a link between the individual and society, between the psychological and the sociological, *between private troubles and public issues*.

Private troubles   These are what individuals worry about: their family, job, prospects of promotion (or unemployment), living conditions. Thus a *trouble* is a private matter for the individual. Sometimes individuals feel threatened, for example by impending unemployment.

Public issues   These are matters that transcend the local environments of the individual. They have to do with the organization of

Table 1.1 Manifest and latent functions

Item	Manifest function	Latent function
Anti-alcohol legislation in the US (prohibition)	To suppress drunkenness	Created illegal outlets for alcohol
Christian missions to parts of Africa	To convert Africans to Christianity	Helped to destroy tribal cultures that held people together
The control of the former Communist Party of the Soviet Union over all sections of social life	The continued dominance of the revolutionary ethos	Created a new crop of comfortable bureaucrats
Schools	To educate the pupils; to teach the 3 'R's; to hand on knowledge	To act as baby minders for mothers; to act as marriage bureaux for some older pupils; to ensure society replicates itself in each generation
Hospitals	To be answered by the reader at the end of the chapter	To be answered by the reader at end of the chapter

Source: Adapted from Merton (1968)

many such milieux into society as a whole, as the following extract indicates.

Unemployment, war, divorce: private troubles or public issues?
Continuing the discussion of the difference between private troubles and public issues, Mills considers a city of 100,000 in which only one person is unemployed. This is his or her personal trouble and in order to solve it we look at the person's character, skills, and so on. However, if in a nation of 50 million 15 million are unemployed we must look beyond the individual: the structure of opportunities has collapsed. Then we must consider, for example, what sort of society would permit this.

Mills goes on to discuss war. The citizens of countries at war have many problems because of the war – for example, how to survive it, or die with honour; how to get a safe position; or even how to make money out of it or how to hasten the end of the war. These are personal values and goals. But the structural issues of war have to do with its causes – what type of people it throws up into a command; its long-term effects on society.

Again, consider marriage. Inside marriage a man and a woman may experience personal troubles, but, when the divorce rate during the first four years of marriage is 250 out of every 1,000 attempts, this is an indication of a structural issue related to the institution of marriage and the family and other institutions that support them (Mills 1970: 14–18).

Peter Worsley: culture and human behaviour

Finally, in this selection of leading sociologists, Peter Worsley (1987) supports the view, advanced earlier, that we are what we are because of what we have learnt rather than what we have inherited, and in this way we learn the role of man or woman.

First, then, human behaviour is strongly influenced by the culture of the society to which we belong. *Culture* consists of the *norms and values* of a society or group (see Glossary). Values are the ultimate goals, beliefs or ends of society. Norms are the approved ways of achieving these ends. Thus in Western societies one of the goals may be the amassing of wealth while the norm may be, say, hard work.

Secondly, although each person is individual, such differences are not solely inherited by our genes. We are also individuals because no two persons are ever exposed to exactly the same set of social experiences. Even identical twins lead different lives and may have different beliefs.

Thirdly, our behaviour, unlike that of animals, is not primarily based on instinct. Rather, as mentioned, our behaviour is based on the social roles we have learnt over a lifetime.

Fourthly, human society can change not because our biology has altered but because our culture changes. Thus we can see how quickly some immigrants to a new country can change their beliefs and behaviour (while other immigrants in the same group do not change and remain in the 'ghetto').

3 Conclusions

- Sociology shows the effect of society on the individual. We are what we have learnt to be. We are learning animals. We learn our social roles from our parents first and then from 'significant others' in our life (a teacher, spouse, etc.). Socialization is an important concept showing how roles are learnt.

- The sociologist *must* show how society really works: he or she must look behind the lace curtains.

- Manifest function refers to outward appearances – what appears to be going on. Latent functions are the hidden activities, which sociologists try to expose.

- The distinction between private troubles and public issues shows the relationship between the individual and society and between psychology and sociology.

- Culture is another important concept in sociology. Culture consists of the norms and values of a society.

Questions

Self-examination questions

(These can be answered from the text.)

What is meant by the following?

- sociology
- lifestyle
- role
- the official view ('of what is going on')
- the unofficial view
- culture

- socialization
- primary socialization
- secondary socialization
- manifest function
- latent function
- private trouble
- public issue

Essay or discussion questions

1   In what ways can the high divorce rate be seen as a public issue?
    Suggestions More is now expected from marriage because, for
    example, of the increasingly impersonal nature of society. As a result
    of this, in turn, couples are less likely to put up with an unsatisfactory
    marriage (see also Hart 1976; Thornes and Collard 1979).

2   Many nurses have poor working conditions. Is this a private trouble
    or a public issue? Give examples.
    Suggestion You could describe briefly the effects of low pay on
    yourself or colleagues (pay for some nurses has increased a little but
    working conditions remain poor). Then show that low pay for women
    (the majority of nurses) persists; for example, reports of the Equal
    Opportunities Commission reveal that women's rate of pay has
    remained two-thirds that of men for the same work. You could discuss
    'sexism' here (see p. 127 and Glossary), and the relationship of the
    professions of doctor and nurse.

3   What did Mills mean by the sociological imagination? What can it do
    for you?
    Suggestion It might be interesting to try to analyse sociologically
    some of the important events in your working life. Follow the rule used
    by Mills, Berger and Merton; for example, what are the manifest and
    latent functions of some of the hospital rules? Perhaps you could
    supply actual examples.

Further Reading

See Bibliography for full details.

P. Berger, *Invitation to Sociology* (1966).
T. Bilton et al., *Introductory Sociology* (1987).
M. Haralambos and M. Holborn, *Sociology: Themes and Perspectives*
    (1990).
M. Joseph, *Sociology for Everyone* (1990).

G. Marshall, *In Praise of Sociology* (1990).
C. Wright Mills, *The Sociological Imagination* (1970).
P. Worsley, *The New Introductory Sociology* (1987).

2 The Professions in Medicine

1 Introduction

Probably two professions that spring to mind as being the most prestigious are those of doctors and lawyers, with the other professions – nursing, accountancy, architecture, teaching – coming below the leading two.

The picture we have of professional people is one that stresses skill and competence; dedication to the task in hand; and high moral standards with an emphasis on duty to the client (or patient).

All this may be true, but the sociologist must look beyond the obvious, as chapter 1 showed, and ask what is really happening. What are the beliefs of these people? What are their ideologies (see Glossary) – if any? What are the manifest and latent functions of the professions? The search for answers to these questions will be conducted by the use of the following concepts: professional socialization, professional ideology and professional power. The central interest will be nursing and other caring professions.

2 Professional Socialization

Socialization has been defined in chapter 1. It refers to the acquisition of the norms and values of the group (or group culture) to which one belongs. In this instance entrants to a profession acquire (or learn, or internalize) the culture of the group – say, the medical profession, or the nursing profession.

Thus on entering a profession students learn far more than the technical skills of the chosen profession. They learn its values, the ideals of the profession and generally how to conduct themselves.

All this is illustrated by a well-known study of a medical school in the USA, *Boys in White* (Becker et al. 1961), in which it was shown that students learnt a lot from each other on informal occasions such as meals and coffee breaks. The students in the case study had a common problem, work overload, and the group seemed to go through a number of stages in dealing with this, by adopting four main perspectives or strategies.

First, there was the long-range perspective of the beginning student – that 'medicine is the best of all professions'. Because of their genuine enthusiasm these students tried to learn everything in the syllabus.

This leads to the initial perspective summed up in the sentence 'It is an effort to learn it all'.

There then follows the provisional perspective, 'You cannot do it all'. Here the students were becoming less idealistic and more calculative. Becker et al. show that it was those students most strongly attached to the student group who were most likely to be in tune with these changing perspectives (and most likely to fare well in the exams).

The final perspective was the most calculating of all – 'What do they want us to know?'

On leaving medical school the students readopted the long-range perspective (medicine was the best of all professions).

Robert Merton, in another well-known study *The Student Physician* (Merton et al. 1957), says that the doctor in his private office is largely subject to the norms and values he has acquired and made his own during his professional socialization at medical school. The medically uninformed patient is not in a position to pass judgement on what the doctor does, while the medically informed colleagues are not in a position to know what is being done. Merton concludes: if correct professional socialization is not thoroughly achieved under the optimum conditions provided by medical school, it is unlikely that it will occur under the less favourable circumstances of private practice.

Turning now to the nursing profession, Ida Harper Simpson describes the professional socialization by which the lay person becomes a professional (1979). She took a sample of some 500 nursing

degree students and monitored their progress from entry to gradu-
ation. The professional institution selects the recruits it wants, and
in this study the students came mainly from small-town America
rather than from the large cities. The students also had similar values,
as table 2.1 indicates.

Thus it seems that the student nurses went into nursing in order
to help others, and Simpson notes they were strikingly unconcerned
with self-expression, competitive achievement and similar values.
They looked forward to helping the patient as a person (and not just
a case). Their interest in nursing was intense, but most of them
looked forward to family life as well. Simpson goes on to contrast
the student ideals of patient care with the bureaucratic nature of
nursing school. To summarize the study, it seems that the recruits
were self-selecting in that they came from a similar social background,
were not competitive, had a strong desire to help people and stuck
to their ideals whatever the influence of the nursing school.

Another well-known study of nursing school is *The Silent Dialogue*
by Olesen and Whittaker (1968), which follows the progress of 479
undergraduate (as distinct from diploma) nursing students through
their course. The main research tool was participant observation, and
they perceived two transitions taking place – from lay person to
graduate and from adolescent to adult.

In a section entitled 'The Art and Practice of "Studentmanship"'

Table 2.1 Values that entering freshmen associated with nursing
(percentages)

Most important consideration in decision to enter nursing	
Extrinsic rewards	18.4
Desire to help people	79.6
Self-expression values	1.9
What is liked best about the work of a nurse	
Being able to help people	68.4
Working with people	22.2
Extrinsic rewards	8.8
Self-expression	0.6
The best description of nursing	
Descriptions of people in nursing	8.1
Descriptions of service to others	88.9
Description of work task	3.0

Source: Adapted from Simpson (1979: 4)

they ask what are the characteristics of the good student. The answer seems to be that they are good at 'psyching out' and 'fronting'. 'Psyching out' means ascertaining what the faculty really wants. Thus 51 per cent said it was important to know when to seek advice; 76 per cent said it was important to be able to understand and discuss one's feelings about the patient with the instructor; 62 per cent said it was important to present new and interesting material about the patient to the instructor (Olesen and Whittaker 1968: 148–53).

'Fronting' means presenting a desirable or 'correct' image to the faculty. (The techniques used in 'fronting' are described in Goffman's (1969) book of essays, *The Presentation of Self in Everyday Life*.)

Both 'psyching out' and 'fronting' are part of the process of professional socialization to becoming a qualified nurse. The title of the book, *The Silent Dialogue*, refers to the student's emerging role and growing self-awareness as a nurse.

The student nurse was constantly seeking confirmation of her role as a nurse; the authors call this *legitimation*. There were a number of different types of legitimation – for example, the sanctioning of the student's claim to the role of nurse, adult or woman. The whole course could be seen as official legitimation.

Then there was non-official legitimation, such as when a patient congratulated the nurse on her work. Underground legitimation occurred in the unofficial encounters between staff and students which confirmed the student in her role as a nurse (Olesen and Whittaker 1968).

Some problems facing the nursing profession

Salvage (1985) draws attention to some of the problems of nurses. Nursing and caring are often regarded as women's work and generally are held in low esteem and are low-paid. It is to be hoped that Project 2000, which aims to make the nursing profession an all-graduate profession, will improve the status, pay and skills of the profession. Salvage feels that nursing should feature *caring* and not just be an extension of the doctor's curing role. At the moment nurses are closely supervised and controlled in their work. There is what sociologists call deskilling and fragmentation of the task and, as in industry and commerce generally, there is too much control by management in the name of so-called *'scientific management'* (see Glossary). In contrast, some authorities have introduced the system of 'nursing process', which emphasizes individualized care for patients.

The nursing process is based on recognition that each patient is an individual. Patients have their own needs, and this should never be forgotten (Salvage 1985: 173). The nursing process is a means of achieving goals based on the patient's needs, but it also encourages systematic assessment of these needs and careful planning, implementation and evaluation of nursing care. Thus in the nursing process the patient should be at the centre of events rather than being one of a production line. All this can encourage the nurse to be more sensitive to the patient's problems and requirements.

Nurses work to exacting standards. However, rather than being accorded true professional status, nurses (or at least the majority who are women) seem to be represented by three images: angels, battleaxes or sex symbols.

The nursing profession is further weakened by the fact that it is deeply split. In Britain the Royal College of Nursing (RCN) is the largest body, claiming some 65 per cent of all nurses in its membership. It states that it will never do anything that could harm the patient and in particular would not strike. The other main body, Unison – formed through a merger of the Confederation of Health Service Employees (COHSE), the National Union of Public Employees (NUPE) and the National and Local Government Officers' Association (NALGO) in July 1993 – is a trade union affiliated to the TUC.

Clay (1987) has said that nursing as a profession has not become politicized. Nurses are confined to their own particular hospital or nursing home, their own specialism, and so on. It might be useful to define two key terms here, *politicization* and *scientific management*.

Politicization is a concept commonly used in sociology and derives partly from Marx, who believed that if large numbers of working-class people came together in the factory they would become aware of their true class position (being oppressed, exploited, etc.). The opposite would apply when workers seldom met or expressed their solidarity. Marx used the term 'false consciousness' to denote the worker's failure to see his or her true class position in society.

A parallel example is the case of married women who are trapped in their own families (Gavron 1983). It was found that these women did not meet together in an organized way, did not become politicized and did not protest.

Turning now to *scientific management*, this was defined by Taylor

(1911), who stressed the need for managers to be fully in charge of the work process. Management, he argued, must say not only what is to be done but how it is to be done at each stage of the work; management was the brain and the workers the hands. The ideology of scientific management is widespread, though it may be called by different names such as 'work study', 'management by objectives', and so on.

Professional ideologies

An ideology is a set of beliefs about the world. Often these beliefs suit the interests of powerful groups in a society such as political parties, big business, the professions and trade unions. These beliefs may give a distorted view of the world – not necessarily completely untrue but perhaps exaggerated.

In his book *The Unmasking of Medicine*, Ian Kennedy (1981) argues that one of the ideologies of the medical profession and to some extent the nursing profession is the belief in cures. As Kennedy puts it, 'we tend to just look for cures and the image created of medicine has increasingly been that of a curing science in which the model of the doctor is that of the engineer/mechanic curing a sick engine. This reaches its high point, in what I see, as an attitude towards death in which dying comes to be regarded as an illness. Call it an illness and you hold out some hope of treatment, control and even cure (Kennedy 1981: 28). All this suggests that the doctor is seen as a dispenser of cures even though many of the diseases that kill us before our time are not curable. In addition the medical profession itself may overlook other aspects such as preventative medicine, health education and improvements in the standard of living including better housing, better diet and less stress, as argued in chapter 6.

Nearly all professions seem to have an ideology. For suggestions regarding the ideologies of architecture, accountancy, law, medicine and nursing, see table 2.2.

To compete successfully with other professions, a profession has, among other things, to socialize its students, to hand on the beliefs (or ideologies) of the profession. Turner (1987) believes the Florence Nightingale image is part of the ideology of the nursing profession, but this image is probably not one the modern nursing profession would want to promote or preserve.

Table 2.2 The ideologies of some professions

	Architecture	Accountancy	Law	Medicine	Nursing
Ideology	Emphasis on creativity and a belief that good surroundings will bring out the best in people	Care and attention to detail	Freedom for all under the law	The cure ideology	Florence Nightingale image and cure ideology
Criticism	Of course architects should be creative but this may get exaggerated. There's a lot of bad architecture in our big impersonal housing estates. There's no evidence that better-designed housing will improve most people – (but a reduction in poverty may help).	Improvement in accountancy techniques are often not followed up, for example, current accounting. Are the professions too cautious?	In England justice is open to all, like the Ritz Hotel (lawyers stress justice, but can the client pay for it?).[a]	Attempts to be too 'scientific'. Perhaps more attention should be given to the patient and to the society which generates and tolerates disease. (See chapters 5 and 6)	Nursing is probably trying to get rid of the Florence Nightingale image. Some nurses seek closer contact with patients and a more collaborative role with doctors.[b]

[a] Source: N. Rees, A Dictionary of Twentieth Century Quotations (Fontana, London, 1987)
[b] Source: Hughes (1988: 7)

Professions and power

Some professions are very powerful, particularly the medical profession. Sociologists are interested in the source of this power and how it is used. The power may be over clients, or its own members, or may influence governments or the public at large.

One trait of the higher professions is that they are concerned with theoretical knowledge (like physiology) and not just skills (for example eye testing).

Another aspect of professionalization is peer review. Only a fellow professional is qualified to judge the quality of the work of a colleague. Thus chapter 7 indicates that doctors are judged by their peers and not by health service managers. Professions also control who is admitted to the profession, their training, the virtual exclusion of outsiders (such as the practitioners of alternative medicine). Professions can be powerful even against governments (especially again the medical profession).

Why does the nursing profession lack power?

Nursing has been called a semi-profession. Etzioni (1969) says there are three main semi-professions, nursing, teaching and social work. These professions have three principal characteristics: they are mainly female, their work is in large bureaucracies and they are poorly paid.

Turner (1987: 149) believes that the failure of nursing to achieve professional autonomy is due to the fact that conflicting demands are made on the nurse or student nurse. These demands come from the career itself, the family, the absence of a strong professional association, and perhaps the lack of continuous commitment to a career to the exclusion of domestic involvements.

Turner argues that the radical stream in the contemporary analysis of nursing has, as a result, been dominated by feminist writers. Nursing is a good example of the subordination of women to *patriarchy* (see Glossary) and the exploitation of women under ideologies which assert that nursing is a natural part of the female personality. Turner says women are exploited as nurses because they are socialized into the female role which equates nursing with mothering and sees the hospital ward as merely an extension of the domestic sphere of labour.

For many writers, the secretary and the nurse are living representatives of the general problem of patriarchy and female subordination. The secretary plays the role of the wife at work, while the nurse plays the role of the mother in hospital (Turner 1987: 149).

3 Conclusions

The study of the professions is very important in understanding medical culture and practice.

The key concept is professional socialization which shows how the ideals and the ideology are passed on to the next generation of students. The ordeals of the course (its work) bind the student to the profession and also bind students to each other – because they share these ordeals. The case study quoted here, *Boys in White* (Becker et al. 1961), demonstrates this point: the students in the group come together to deal with the stress from which they all suffer – work overload.

The Merton study (Merton et al. 1957) demonstrates how beliefs instilled at college last a lifetime and guide the practitioners when they are on their own.

The Simpson (1979) study of nursing students confirms the findings on the importance of professional socialization. In addition Simpson shows the importance of prior socialization in that most students arrive at the doors of the nursing school already imbued with the values (and ideologies) of the nursing profession.

In *The Silent Dialogue* Olesen and Whittaker (1968) try to capture what goes on in the student's mind during the process of professionalization. They show that the 'good' student does not just learn technical facts, but also learns the techniques of fronting and psyching out and in this way internalizes the norms and values of his or her chosen profession.

Finally, the nature of professional power and professional ideology was discussed in order, among other things, to answer the question: what is necessary to make nursing a stronger profession?

Questions

Self-examination questions

(The answers are in the text.)

What is meant by the following?

- socialization
- professional socialization
- ideologies
- professional ideologies
- power
- professional power
- norms

- values
- psyching out
- fronting
- legitimation
- 'cure'
- preventative medicine

Essay or discussion questions

1 In view of her good work, what is wrong in the nursing profession's having a Florence Nightingale image or ideology?
   Suggestion This ideology seems to work in favour of the powerful – the employers, governments and those at the top of the nursing profession who may use this image to appeal to nurses to accept lower wages, suggesting that the truly caring nurse would never go on strike.

2 What is a semi-profession and what distinguishes it from a full profession?
   Suggestion Nursing, teaching and social work tend to be semi-professions. These professions are mainly female, relatively low paid, and work in large organizations such as hospitals, schools and local authorities. They are a long way from the image of the high-status, independent practitioner such as a doctor (Etzioni 1969).

3 Read the extract and answer the questions that follow.

> The Age of Professions will be remembered as the time when politics withered, when voters, guided by professionals, entrusted to technocrats the power to legislate needs, renounced the authority to decide who needs what and suffered monopolistic oligarchies to determine the means by which these needs shall be met. It will be remembered as the age of schooling, when people for one-third of their lives had their learning needs prescribed and were trained how to accumulate further needs, and for the other two-thirds became clients of prestigious pushers who managed their habits. It will be remembered as the age when recreational travel meant a packaged gawk at strangers, and intimacy meant following the sexual rules laid down by Masters and Johnson and their kind; when informed opinion was a replay of last night's TV talk-show, and voting the approval of persuaders and salesmen for more of the same (from Illich 1977: 12–13).

(a) What is Illich complaining about?
(b) What criticism would you make of his 'complaints'?

Suggestions He seems to be complaining about 'experts' (i.e. professionals) taking over the world. The experts will render the rest of us helpless, hence the title of the book, *Disabling Professions. But* it could be counter-argued that Illich is harking back to some idyllic past when we could all attend to our simple needs. What do you think?

---

4 How can knowledge of this chapter help nurses in their work?
   Attempt this question on your own or in a group first before reading the suggestions here.

Suggestions
(a) This chapter and the next help to show where power resides in a hospital – with the doctors and consultants.
(b) The chapter shows the importance of professional socialization and anticipatory socialization (before even reaching nursing school), e.g. a family background of nursing or medicine.

(c) Sociology helps to analyse ideologies, for example professional ideologies like the 'cure' ideology in medicine and nursing. Most professions have ideologies.

(d) people in organizations like hospitals perform roles (see also chapters 3 and 7). Thus the doctor has a role and so has a nurse. So too has the patient. Sociology helps the nurse to understand the patient's role as well as his or her own.

---

5   Examine the three case studies and answer the questions that follow.

Case study 1

A heated argument broke out in the kitchen one day. One auxiliary wanted to 'do the teas' as usual (milk, sugar, tea, all in one pot because it was quicker). Both approached the ward charge nurse to do a 'judgement of Solomon'! 'We're busy, we've got to get on,' said one. 'But we talked about our philosophy last week, we all agreed that the patients have choice – is this giving them choice?' The patients got a choice of drinks that day and henceforth. Consensus of what is better for patients rather than what is quicker for the nurse can be a powerful stimulus to change.

Case study 2

It's 4 p.m. It had been the tradition of the ward to start putting patients back to bed, so that all were in bed for the evening.

A student nurse suggests 'It seems to me, they all go to bed because they think we want it.'

'I agree,' replies an auxiliary. 'But the trouble is, if we don't get done quickly, the night staff complain if they're not in bed.'

'Well, we'll have a meeting with the night staff tonight,' replies the charge nurse, 'we need to have a look at their point of view, but I'm sure we can work something out.'

'I've tried asking the patients, but it's difficult, they seem to think I want them back in bed, so I suspect they say yes just to please me' (student nurse).

'What do you think?' (charge nurse to auxiliary).

'Well,' she replies, 'maybe if we just don't ask, and leave it up to them to tell us, and we should keep an eye on them to see if any look uncomfortable or restless.'

By late afternoon, patients are watching the news on TV. Some are walking about, other have taken friends outdoors. Two patients are still watching football on TV at 11.05 p.m. That night there is a meeting with night staff, the next day, a quick discussion to re-appraise the situation. It seemed like a good idea. The night nurse felt the patients slept better. Two patients whom she expected to be incontinent were not. One patient complained – 'Why is there only one bloody TV?'

Case study 3

An acute surgical ward sister has developed a philosophy and is trying to change the nursing approach.

'This model stuff you talk about won't work here, we haven't got the staff.'

'What do you need staff for, don't you want to change anything? Does nursing always need more people to do things? How about just giving your ideas a try?'

The patients on the ward tend to wear night clothes all day.

'I've often wondered why we do this – makes it easier for the doctors to examine them I suppose? I think we'll start with that.'

Next morning, sister and her nurse suggest that more than half the patients put their own clothes on. Some look surprised, others make positive comments – 'I feel quite human in my own things.' The doctor looks puzzled but says little, except 'It's a bother fiddling with buttons' (from Wright 1986: 26).

(a) What is happening in these case studies?
(b) What can be learned from them?
(c) How far do these studies apply to your hospital? Give as many actual examples as possible.

Suggestions
• Some wards seem to be run in a rigid way.

- Patients need independence.
- Compare hospitals with other large organizations using material in this book (chapters 3 and 7).

---

6   Read this passage and answer the questions that follow.

Schools for Scandal

Most students come out of medical school without knowing any first aid.

If you're starting at medical school this term, full of intellectual passion for the art and science of medicine, then I sympathise, I really do. You are about to discover that medicine is one of the worst taught subjects in the whole of the British University curriculum. I've not met a single British doctor who didn't think a large part of his or her undergraduate education was a total waste of time.

What most non-medics know about medical education is that the course is very long and arduous. This is a source of pride to doctors, which betrays the fact that we view medical school not as a learning experience but as a rite of passage – a kind of intellectual survival course, designed not to inspire you about the subject of medicine but to test your mental endurance to its very limit. Army recruits are trained in exactly the same way. It is despite, rather than because of the training that the army or the medical profession occasionally throws up a caring free-thinking individual.

Many doctors emerge brutalised. A General Medical Council report due to be published later this year laments the 'progressive disenchantment of many students' in the course of their education, and blames the mindless, uncritical cramming they are obliged to do. I can still remember, with a chill of horror, sitting up all night with an anatomy textbook trying to make sense of the three dimensional anatomy of the base of the neck. It took me a week to learn my way through this maze and about half-an-hour to forget it in the Union bar after the exam.

The idea behind this rote-learning is that you have to learn the basic science before you can progress to clinical work. But most other university departments have tumbled to the fact that the basics are what you teach last, after the students have a firm grip on the relevance of the subject. You don't teach about Rembrandt's brushwork before you explain who Rembrandt was. You don't teach about Shakespeare's sentence construction before you've seen a play (from John Collee, *Observer*, 16 August 1992).

(a) What is wrong with medical school as described here?
(b) What might a sociologist be interested in in this extract?

Suggestions
- The concept of professional socialization may be interesting here.
- Stress that at medical school students may learn more than technical facts and in the same way this may be true of nursing school.

Further Reading

See Bibliography for full details.

H. Becker et al., *Boys in White* (1961).
H. Braverman, *Labour and Monopoly Capital* (1974).
T. Clay, *Nurses: Power and Politics* (1987).
I. Kennedy, *The Unmasking of Medicine* (1981).
L. Mackay, *Nursing a Problem* (1989).
V. L. Olesen and E. W. Whittaker, *The Silent Dialogue* (1968).
I. H. Simpson, *From Student to Nurse* (1979).
F. W. Taylor, *The Principles of Scientific Management* (1911).
B. S. Turner, *Medical Power and Social Knowledge* (1987).
S. G. Wright, *Building and Using a Model of Nursing* (1986).
S. G. Wright, *Changing Nursing Practice* (1990).

3 The Hospital as an Organization: Beliefs and Realities

1 Introduction

- What would a perfectly run organization look like?
- What would a perfectly run hospital look like?
- How far does the average hospital fall short of a perfectly run organization?

These are some of the topics discussed in this chapter, which also looks at:

- The place of professionals in hospitals.
- Communications in the hospital.
- The hospital as an arena where conflicting beliefs compete.
- The hospital as an arena where professionals co-operate and teams work smoothly together.
- The hospital as an asylum.

Overall the sociologist would see the hospital as an organization having many of the features of any other organization such as schools, prisons, armies and large commercial firms. For example, there may be a clear hierarchy of office (some jobs are ranked higher than others); the members of staff are required to fulfil the duties of their own job only; outside the work they are free to do whatever they want; each position has a clearly specific job description (they know what they have to do at work). The danger here is that while standardization produces bureaucratic efficiency it can lead to depersonalization too (Turner 1987).

2 Beliefs and Realities in the Hospital

The major contribution that sociologists can make to the study of hospitals is to show that they are not always rational scientific organizations but are affected by ideologies (see Glossary).

Perhaps the hospital could be divided into four main groups – the managers, the doctors, the nurses and the patients. Each group has its own ideologies or beliefs. Thus on visiting, or working in, a hospital you may find that the managers and administrators adhere to a belief in 'scientific management' (see Glossary) which says that management must fully control the situation at all stages.

The doctors may stress the importance of 'cures' at the expense of other ways of dealing with illness. It is not that a belief in 'cures' is wrong but that it excludes other ways of thinking of the problems. The doctor's viewpoint may differ markedly from that of the managers. The doctors may, for example, require expensive equipment or more staff, while managers may seek more efficiency and greater value for money. The doctors require most of all clinical freedom, while the managers require control of the organization. This will be demonstrated by case studies later.

The nurses again may have a different ideology. It was suggested in chapter 2 that the nursing profession may still have a Florence Nightingale ideology, with a strong emphasis on caring. This may be a good thing, but it is exploited by other groups competing in the hospital. In the end it may result in nurses getting poor working conditions generally.

Finally there are the patients themselves, the most numerous and the weakest group in the hospital. One reason they are weak is that they do not come together as a group; hence they are unorganized and do not become politicized.

3 The Hospital as a Total Institution

It may be useful to study the hospital using Goffman's (1968) idea
of a total institution. The total institution is a place where a large
number of people come together and where they are relatively cut
off from the wider society – for example, prison, the army, the
religious seminary, the military academy, the mental hospital and the
secure hospital. On admission to the total institution, the inmates
have their old values stripped away and they are introduced to a new
regime where they have a role (patient, prisoner, etc.) and new
expected behaviour. A version of this process was described in chapter 2
when the nature of professional socialization for doctors and nurses
was discussed.

Of course a nursing school, for example, may not seem to be total
institution, yet all the examples quoted here do have some features
of the total institution (Goffman 1968).

Consider the following conversation, taken from Brendan Behan's
Borstal Boy.

Admission to a total institution
'And, 'old up your 'ead, when I speak to you.'
"Old up your 'ead, when Mr Whitbread speaks to you,' said
Mr Holmes.
I looked round at Charlie. His eyes met mine and he quickly
lowered them to the ground.
'What are you looking round at, Behan? Look at me.'

*   *   *

I looked at Mr Whitbread. 'I am looking at you,' I said.
'You are looking at Mr Whitbread – what?' said Mr Holmes.
'I am looking at Mr Whitbread.'
Mr Holmes looked gravely at Mr Whitbread, drew back his
open hand, and struck me on the face, held me with his other
hand and struck me again.
My head spun and burned and pained and I wondered would
it happen again. I forgot and felt another smack, and forgot,
and another, and moved, and was held by a steadying, almost

kindly hand, and another, and my sight was a vision of red and white and pity-coloured flashes.

'You are looking at Mr Whitbread – what, Behan?'

I gulped and got together my voice and tried again till I got out, 'I, sir, please, sir, I am looking at you, I mean I am looking at Mr Whitbread, sir' (Behan 1964: 41).

This is obviously an extreme example of a total institution and its admission procedures. A sociologist might want to ask: how far does this hospital/prison/school resemble a total institution? What are its admission procedures? A case study is considered towards the end of this chapter.

4 Effects of Hospitalization

Envisaging the hospital as a total institution may be helpful in studying the effects of hospitalization. Scambler (1991: 65) suggests three main effects of hospitalization. First there is stress: the patient is worried because the future is now uncertain and the hospital routines seem strange. There is a strong fear of the unknown both in the hospital and in the future generally. Secondly there is depersonalization: a third of patients in a case study complained of being regarded as just another case rather than as individuals. Lack of privacy was another complaint. Then there is institutionalization. Long-term patients may become apathetic and be unable to perform simple tasks. They may lack autonomy and self-identity. Here it could be asked what the role of the nurse is in dealing with the worse effects of hospitalization.

Staff should talk to patients more often and more deeply. It would be useful to have an explanatory booklet prior to admission (although a Royal Commission of 1976 found that only 59 per cent of discharged patients had reported having been given such a book). Once institutionalization occurs, attempts must be made to provide a more stimulating environment – easier said than done in the case of the mentally handicapped, for example. Really it depends on our values as a society. Are we genuinely concerned? If so, why do we not do more for the mentally handicapped? Why do we object to their living in our street?

5   A Role for Doctors on the Management Scene

The Griffiths Report on management in hospitals in the UK (DHSS 1983) recommended that doctors should be looked upon as natural managers and that general management should become part of their training.

However, Smith, Makinson and Farrow (1986) showed that what doctors wanted most was clinical freedom, not managerial responsibility. But doctors were making decisions all the time – for example, on the allocation of resources – and medical school should give students the chance to improve their management skills.

A report by the Institute of Health Service Management looked at how clinicians can help managers to make decisions on the best use of resources. It was felt that doctors should become more involved in decisions on resource allocation. Their relationship has to be one of working together to achieve a common end. The following remarks summarize the report (see Disken 1990).

Clinical management: the essentials

- Timely and accurate information about the performance of clinical services must be made available.

- Whatever the clinical management infrastructure, there must be clinical leadership.

- The organizational model must be carefully thought through and clearly described at the outset.

- Above all, it is essential that doctors and managers understand each other's role and responsibility better – a message which applies not only to clinical management but to a whole host of issues affecting the health service.

It could be concluded that there are two types of authority in hospital: the professional authority of the doctors; and the managerial authority of the higher managers.

6 Some Guidelines for Research in Health Service Organizations

Hunter (1990) has suggested some areas of management suitable for sociological research into the nature of health organizations, especially health organizations.

(a) *Environment*   A problem applicable to most large organizations is goal displacement, whereby, for example, the organization has one goal and its members another; some members of the health service may be acting in accordance with the business society ethics, while others may stress the medical point of view; some might spend too much time on record-keeping so that reports, memoranda and meetings become ends in themselves; finally *some* organizations seem to be run for the convenience of the staff rather than the customers, clients, patients and consumers. Do you notice these problems in your own organization?

(b) *Improved management performance*   It is difficult to measure the effectiveness of management, especially in the health service. There are different styles of management, for example the open-door style whereby the manager is always available for consultation. However, there is little evidence to show one style is more effective than another. Perhaps performance indicators could be used. Thus a researcher could ask: are managers doing what they think they are doing? What exactly is the manager's role here? What is the link (if there is one) between what managers are doing and what the organization is achieving?

(c) *Medical technology and innovation*   How does new technology affect the health organization? In what circumstances will new technology be introduced? New technology is not just a technical matter. Rather one should ask in what sort of society new technology is used. Thus the decision to use new technology is also a cultural one. Again this is an under-researched area. What new technology has your hospital (or organization) introduced? Was it a success? How do you measure its success? Is it proposed to introduce any further technology?

(d) *Internal organizational relationships*   The relationship between clinicians and managers has been touched on elsewhere in this book. It may be a good idea to fuse the relations between clinicians and managers. Would patient care suffer, or would it be improved? Does clinical freedom denote a special type of one-to-one relationship that should not be lightly jettisoned? Probably the answer to the last question is 'yes'. Doctors have great professional power (as chapter 2 showed) and they will assert their clinical freedom.

Hunter concludes his remarks on health service research by saying research should aim at explaining behaviour in health service organizations. Researchers should pay less attention to the formal structure of organizations and more to the structure of power at all levels of the national health service. Research should be for a purpose; thus research and policy should be closely linked. Medical sociology should illuminate organizational life generally (see Hunter 1990: 230–4).

Some general criticism could be made here. C. Wright Mills in *The Sociological Imagination* argues that we should not accept management's definition of problems but rather should seek a sociological definition. Thus, instead of asking, for example, 'How can output be increased?', a sociologist might ask 'How can we attend more to what patients say?'

Again, rather than ask 'How can we improve the productivity of these nurses?' the sociologist might ask 'Are these nurses alienated in their work?' (Alienation was a term used by Marx to show that in so far as people do not express their true creative selves through their work they are alienated.)

7   Conclusions

One way to conclude this chapter is to consider how a sociologist distinguishes between beliefs and reality in the administration of the health service. This is attempted in table 3.1.

Table 3.1 Beliefs and reality in the administration of the health services

Beliefs	Reality
(a) The hospital is a rational organization pursuing rational goals (good health for the patients) by rational means (good medical practice).	The hospital comprises groups of people, each group having its own beliefs and ideologies.
(b) Patients may come into hospital because they want the doctor to cure them.	'Cures' are of course important but there may be better ways to health in the long run such as better diet and better lifestyles generally.
(c) Medicine by its very nature requires strict discipline.	This is true but the hospital must not become a total institution. People must treat each other with respect. Initiation must not be too shocking.
(d) Doctors should join with managers in running the hospitals, etc.	Doctors do not want to be managers; they want clinical freedom, as several case studies have shown.
(e) The manifest function of the hospital is to cure the sick, and to carry out appropriate medical procedures.	One latent function of the hospital may be to socialize the seriously ill to their fate, whether it is dying or a lifetime of personal disablement; to apply the medical model which stresses the importance of the scientific and hence medical view; and to try to make life as normal as possible in the face of disease (note that many big hospitals have a hospital shop, a hospital cafeteria, a hospital radio, etc.).
(f) Sociologists should make themselves more useful and help managers with their problems.	Sociologists should try to understand what is actually going on – in this hospital or that school. Who has the power? Whose ideologies prevail?

Questions

Self-examination questions

(These can be answered from the book.)

What is meant by the following?

- professional autonomy
- clinical independence (or clinical freedom)
- ideology

- cure ideology
- politicization
- asylum
- total institution

Essay or discussion questions

1   How near does your hospital (or employing organization) come to a rational organization? Give actual examples.

2   How near does your hospital (or employing organization) come to Goffman's total institution? Give actual examples. (see Glossary).

3   What is meant by scientific management? Can you supply some actual examples?
Suggestions   See chapter 2 for a definition of scientific management (and see Glossary); seek examples from hospitals and any other organizations with which you are familiar.

4   It seems (from studies quoted here) that doctors are reluctant to take on a managerial role in hospitals and in the NHS generally. Why is this? Does it matter? What would you say doctors really wanted?
Suggestions   Use the studies quoted here and evidence from your work place. See also chapter 7.

5   As a sociologist what would you say is going on here? What should be done?

The pit and the pendulum: an inside story

Sholom Glouberman has recorded a dozen interviews with workers in maximum security prisons, long-stay hospitals, homes, and other 'total' institutions for his new book, *Keepers*. Exploring the relationships between the workers and patients or inmates, they provide a remarkable insight into these closed environments and the people within them. One is printed here . . .

'. . . Patients can ask for a lot from you. You have to really listen to them. Listen to them, it will do them some good. People sit in a chair here all day, waiting for someone to just talk to them, to wash them, to give them their food. It's hard for them. They are aware of what is happening. They know everything. They have to sit and wait for everything in this hospital. They have to wait for the world to come to them. They are very involved in all that. I come here, I work, and then I go home. Here they are surrounded by the hospital. And they see death. I do too, but they are waiting for it. No one comes in here and later leaves. They come in and they die.

After some years of working here you feel that too. You say "My God, what is life after all? Everything you do is hard. You go to school. It's hard. You work. It's hard." Then you see those people and you think "I could wake up some morning and catch some sickness, some virus." It's a wheel that turns. The years go by, centuries follow centuries, and it's all the same. Every one will die.

Some people have more to them than others. They develop their talents more. They grow. Others don't. Some have more wealth, they can travel more than you and me, more than ordinary people. In my work you can't do too much because you don't have a big salary. But you can make as much of a life as anyone, as much as a big doctor. He might be able to do a big operation and save someone's life. But even that can be routine. Maybe I am not a professional, and I don't save anyone's life. So people think that what I do must be easy. But it isn't, it's hard. My work is also routine up to a certain point . . . .' (from S. Glouberman, interview with worker in long-stay hospital, *Guardian*, 16 January 1991).

Suggestions
- Use the work of Goffman and especially his concept of the total institution.

- How do you avoid institutionalization?
- Perhaps discuss the view that as a society we get the sort of total institution we deserve.
- What role can the nurse play in all this? (See chapter 3, section 4.)

---

6   A new patient is to be admitted to an acute ward. What are the correct procedures and what is the aim of these procedures? What improvements would you suggest? You could set this up as a role-play exercise with two main characters: the ward sister or charge nurse and a new in-patient. A script could be prepared for both these roles. Preferably have more than one pair (so that each pair may criticize the other).

---

7   Read the extract and answer the questions that follow.

The abuse of power in a rotten culture

Sir Louis Blom-Cooper QC must feel he's supped full of horrors. He has now presided over three inquiries into how the caring system manifestly fails to protect its vulnerable charges. In the process, he has heard enough details of the unspeakable cruelties people inflict upon battered children in particular.

Yet his latest report, following the public inquiry into ill-treatment at Ashworth special hospital, is particularly upsetting. Some of its images stay in the mind like a haunting. The cruelty, the beatings, the mysterious deaths, the utterly inadequate treatment, they're all hard enough to stomach, not least because here is a hospital, an allegedly therapeutic institution, where staff actually inflicted pain and torment on their patients in a regime which (hopefully) wouldn't even be tolerated in a prison. But there's another dimension to this which makes it almost intolerable to read.

When the Holocaust survivor Elie Wiesel tried to commit suicide years after the horror he had experienced, he explained that the cause of his despair was not the torments that had been inflicted upon him but the indifference of the world to what had happened, the refusal to believe and the instinct to minimise. It is that factor of indifference to cruelty or, even worse, apparent connivance at it that is such a powerful thread running through the Ashworth report and that makes it so hard to stomach. The nursing staff, or a large section of it, ran a brutal regime in which they tormented patients not just by physical ill-treatment, and there was enough of that too, but by psychological abuse which they regarded as a joke. After all, if you're terrifying someone by a severed pig's head, or by sending them a snake in a package, or by using them as a human ash-tray by tipping cigarette ash inside the waistband of their trousers, it's all tremendously funny if you start from the premise that these patients are a kind of sub-human species, an assumption which appears to have been implicit in the behaviour of these nurses. The patients − or rather, victims − in these vicious anecdotes come across as infinitely pathetic, sometimes too ill to understand the degradation that was being perpetrated upon them. It is a shocking chronicle of a wholesale abuse of power (from Melanie Phillips, *Guardian*, 7 August 1992).

How far is Ashworth Special Hospital a total institution? Give other examples of total institutions, especially from those who are familiar with one. Why is the nursing profession apparently so quiet about Ashworth? What needs to be done? What is the government doing?

Suggestions
- See Goffman (1968).
- The 'management' in a total institution demand a monopoly in defining the meaning of the institution and what goes on inside.
- The 'inmates' have no contact with the 'outside'.
- Perhaps it ought to be made easier for the inmates, the staff and the public to complain.

Further Reading

See Bibliography for full details.

D. Armstrong, *An Outline of Sociology as Applied to Medicine* (1983b).
E. Goffman, *Asylums* (1968).

D. Hunter, 'Organizing and Managing Health Care' (1990).
D. Hunter and K. Judge, *Griffiths and Community Care: Meeting the Challenge* (1988).
M. Morgan, M. Calnan and N. Manning, *Sociological Approaches to Health and Medicine* (1985).
Royal Commission on the National Health Service, *Patients' Attendance to the Hospital Service* (HMSO, London, 1976).
G. Scambler (ed.), *Sociology as Applied to Medicine* (1991).
G. J. Smith, D. H. Makinson and S. C. Farrow, 'Learning to Swim with the Griffiths Tide' (1986).
B. S. Turner, *Medical Power and Social Knowledge* (1987).

4 Relationships in the Health Services

1 Introduction

This chapter analyses relationships in the health services and asks whether there is good communication between doctor and patient. If not, why not? Any regular contact between two or three or more people can be regarded as a relationship. This could include mother and child, husband and wife, doctor and patient, teacher and pupils, and so on. We are therefore surrounded by relationships; we live in relationships; indeed we are born in a relationship.

Accordingly this chapter analyses some of the more important human relationships in medicine including the doctor–patient relationship and the doctor–nurse relationship. The chapter begins with an explanation of the 'sick role' and ends with the social role of medicine in society.

2 The Sick Role

One concept that may be useful in the analysis of relationships is that of the sick role. Here the patient is allowed to withdraw from the world, so to speak, while the doctor is expected to apply his or her skills in a detached, scientific way (see chapter 2 and Glossary for a definition of *role*). Table 4.1 explains what is meant by the sick role. It might be interesting to see how far it can be used in the other relationships described later in this chapter.

Table 4.1   Parsons's analysis of the roles of patients and doctors

Patient: sick role	*Doctor: professional role*
Obligations and privileges	*Expected to*
1 Must want to get well as quickly as possible.	1 Apply a high degree of skill and knowledge of the problems of illness.
2 Should seek professional medical advice and co-operate with the doctor.	2 Act for the welfare of patient and community rather than for own self-interest, desire for money, advancement, etc.
3 Allowed (and may be expected) to shed some normal activities and responsibilities (e.g. employment, household tasks).	3 Be objective and emotionally detached (i.e. should not judge patients' behaviour in terms of personal value systems or become emotionally involved with them).
4 Regarded as being in need of care and unable to get better by his or her own decision and will.	4 Be guided by rules or professional practice.
	Rights
	1 Granted right to examine patients physically and to enquire into intimate areas of physical and personal life.
	2 Granted considerable autonomy in professional practice.
	3 Occupies position of authority in relation to the patient.

Source: Adapted from Parsons (1951)

3   The Doctor–Patient Relationship

Scambler (1991) says that, although there may be little outward conflict between doctor and patient, doctors and patients may try to influence each other in a number of ways, such as the use of persuasion. Thus the patient may calculate what the consultant wants to hear; for example, in a study of ENT clinics, patients commonly mentioned the GP's diagnosis (Bloor 1976). Patients try to reach a compromise with the doctor. This is easiest when there is uncertainty as to the cause of their condition (Roth 1963). Even when there is no uncertainty about outcomes, doctors may prolong uncertainty to increase their power (Davis 1960). Where a doctor is apparently not paying attention, shuffling notes perhaps, the patients may lose interest and not disclose symptoms (Bloor 1976).

Some people fail to see the doctor despite experiencing serious symptoms, while others frequently see the doctor with minor complaints. Armstrong estimates one-third to one-half within the latter category (Armstrong 1983b). How far is this decision to consult or not a rational decision?

The experience of symptoms

Symptoms are very common, though most are transient and are soon forgotten. The meaning placed on the symptoms can vary according to the patient's mood; it is not so much the actual symptom which influences the patient's behaviour but the meaning placed on it. For example, in an experiment people were asked to keep health diaries, but many withdrew from the experiment because they claimed that recording the symptoms made them feel ill (Armstrong 1983b: 5). This seems to indicate that the experience of symptoms is not purely a biological matter. Thus symptoms can be thought serious by the patient but not by the doctor, and vice versa. (See also chapter 6, 'A Social Construction of Illness'.)

Illness behaviour   Before deciding to see the doctor, patients had asked themselves 'Are my symptoms normal?' Symptoms may be classified as normal merely because they are common, for example headaches. The ailments of old age may come to be regarded as normal for the elderly – 'what can you expect at my age?' Similarly a cough may come to be regarded as normal 'when it's only a smoker's cough'.

Interactions of doctors, patients and their families

How do doctors interact with patients and patients' families? In a study of fifteen families in which a child suffered renal failure (Waissman 1990), one aim was to keep parents informed of treatment. The treatment a child was to receive was discussed, but it was often a one-sided discussion, since the doctor had the resources, the drugs, the expertise, and so on.

On the other hand, the parents were encouraged to take part in the treatment, learn to use the dialysis machine, and to prepare the daily diet. The doctors aimed to keep parents fully informed of the treatment, but parents often forgot what happened at these meetings. Again the information was not always understood by parents.

The following is a brief summary of Waissman's article.

The 'normalisation' of everyday life was a value shared by doctors and parents. It orientated and shaped the plans that parents made. A recurrent theme in interviews was their imagined occupation for the sick child when he was adult. This theme reveals not only the hope that he will live and grow up, but also concern about planning his future. Home dialysis is an important step before kidney transplant, a step that prepares the child for this new ordeal, which, for the parents as for the doctors, is the only means that may enable him to lead a nearly normal life.

Some sociological comments may be considered:

- The aim of the treatment is said to be the normalization of everyday life, and arguably it is no coincidence that this is similar to Goffman's (1969) book of essays, *The Presentation of Self in Everyday Life*.

- The study shows that life can be extended by technology but that ultimately it is the quality of life that matters most. (What sort of occupation could these patients look forward to in this example?)
- The doctor, in representing the medical profession, is ultimately in charge of the relationship.
- As mentioned, the doctor's instructions were sometimes incomprehensible to the parents, who in turn often forgot what the doctor had said. Perhaps the underlying reason for this lack of communication is that people from different backgrounds cannot communicate easily with each other.
- The effect on the rest of the family is important. Often it seems the welfare workers want the parents to 'cope' (cope is a 'good' word). (But is the encouragement to 'cope' in everyone's interest – or is the emphasis on coping just a means of saving money for the health service?)

The 'disabled' role

According to a study by Lonsdale (1990), more than 3.5 million women in Britain are disabled. The way in which the women defined the nature of their disability differed from that of the doctors. Medical services cast these women in a passive role in which things are done to them. The health culture sees doctors as curers. Usually the disabled try to participate in as normal a lifestyle as soon as possible rather than strive against the disability in a fruitless attempt to be able-bodied.

Thus one young woman with cerebral palsy reported that her special school had given priority to her medical treatment over her general education, which would have made it easier to make her way in the world. 'Adaptation' is more important than chasing 'cures'.

Looking at Lonsdale's study from a sociological view, there seems to be a 'disabled' *role* which the disabled person is expected to adopt (similar in principle to the adoption of the sick role – see section 2). The disabled role stresses passivity, docility and dependence. This would be 'good' role behaviour. 'Bad' role behaviour would comprise striving to be independent. In time, some of the disabled are socialized to act the disabled role, while others strive to maintain their independence.

Complementary medicine: a sociological view

The medical profession, according to Freidson (1986), is a large organization with a monopoly in the practice of medicine. There are signs that fringe medicines (including healing, acupuncture, etc.) would tend to move in this way. Thus complementary medicine may develop a body of knowledge, an ideology or set of beliefs and would patrol the boundaries of its work to keep out 'unqualified' intruders. In so doing it would come to act increasingly like conventional medicine.

4   The Consultant–Patient Relationship

Continuing the theme of relationships in the health services, the consultant–patient relationship is now examined, starting with a few common questions.

Should patients have access to their medical records? Why do consultants withhold information? Can patients have an informed relationship with consultants? These were the questions asked by Britten (1986) using a sample of twenty-four hospitals. One important finding was that consultants opposed to access to records held to a bio-medical model of illness, whereas those in favour of access held to a more psycho-social model of illness.

In the bio-medical model, illness is reduced to a biological abnormality within the body. Communication is usually one way – from the consultant to patient. The patient is not perceived as wanting information. Thus there is no good reason for patients to see their own records.

In psycho-social models the patients are regarded as 'human beings' with thoughts and feelings rather than just a biological abnormality. If the patients' feelings are acknowledged, it follows that patients have a valid contribution to make to the consultation over and above supplying details of their condition. Again, in the psycho-social model of illness information flows both up and down.

It seems that consultants have strong views on the disclosure of information. Thus one consultant pointed out the disadvantage of allowing patients access to their records: 'You won't be able to write down things like "God only knows". Under the present system I can immediately orient myself towards the patient, for example if I see the words "What a wally".'

The following conclusions could possibly be drawn with regard to the patient–consultant relationship:

- First, medical notes may have to be more clearly written for patients to see.

- Secondly, it could become a human right to see your medical records.

- Thirdly, perhaps the consultant and patient should have an informed relationship.

- Finally, this may become an increasingly important issue. People are living longer and may suffer increasingly from chronic diseases such as diabetes. (This makes it even more important that the consultant should be able to converse with the patient and vice versa.)

As mentioned earlier, when seeing the doctor a patient's first question – spoken or unspoken – is 'Am I normal doctor?' In replying, the doctor may consider (a) whether the patient is normal from a physiological viewpoint and (b) whether the patient is normal from a social viewpoint. Table 4.2 gives a few examples.

5 Conclusions

Relationships In this chapter it is argued that we all play our roles within relationships and that in the health services the main relationship is that between doctor and patient.

Within these relationships it is usual that one side has more power than another; for example, the doctor has more power than the nurse. These distortions lead to problems such as poor communication and failure to understand the treatment. However, it is wrong to give the impression that doctors, consultants, etc., are always in tension. Usually teams work smoothly.

Sociology is particularly useful in tracking down these problems, as chapters 5 and 6 show.

Table 4.2 The doctor–patient relationship and the social role of medicine in society

Presenting complaint	Doctor's action	A sociological view
A patient breaks a leg.	The doctor treats the complaint physically.	A broken leg will be recognized as much by the doctor as by the patient as a condition requiring treatment.
A patient feels tired and wants to be excused work.	The doctor examines the patient, finds nothing wrong and declines to give a sick note.	The widely held social view is that people should work. We often feel guilty if we are not working. Is it true? Why is this so?
A patient complains of acne.	The doctor gives a prescription.	The doctor agreed with the patient's view that the marks left are socially undesirable. In his book *Stigma*, Goffman (1990) argues that the physically deformed person must constantly strive to adjust to his or her precious social identity. We (the 'normal' people) tend to notice the stigma before noticing the person. We confirm the stigma whether by rejecting the stigmatized person or whether by over-hearty acceptance.

A patient complains of insomnia for two nights.	The doctor decides to give sleeping tablets.	Sleeping pills may put us to sleep sociologically. We feel alienated at work and frustrated in the family. Indeed, for many the family may act as a sort of prison (Gavron 1983). The doctor who prescribes the sleeping pill or tranquillizer is perpetuating the alienation in society, yet not to prescribe it may be considered cruel.
A patient presents with excessive sputum.	The doctor diagnoses chronic bronchitis.	Bronchitis is strongly correlated to poor living conditions at home and at work. Bronchitis is also associated with cigarette smoking, which in turn is closely associated with social class; working-class people smoke more, and this in turn may be due to more stress again (see chapter 6). *Note* The rate of bronchitis could be taken as an indicator of working-class health.
A patient requests that a doctor withholds treatment for a terminal illness.	The doctor may refuse this request.	First, life is held sacred in Western society. Secondly, as chapter 2 showed, the socialization of medical students is long and detailed, emphasizing the importance of curing the disease. Some say the patient's wishes should be respected and death granted (provided the patient was rational at the time of making this request).

Source: Adapted from Armstrong (1983b: 77–9)

Roles   According to Goffman (1969), we all play roles throughout our lives, we present ourselves to society, and we are socialized to these roles throughout our lives, especially in childhood. Society has given us our roles – doctor, patient, sick role, etc. – and we as actors can perform the role (some better than others).

Behaviour is neither random nor fully controlled. Thus it is important in sociological analyses not to see the doctor solely as an individual but rather as a socialized actor on a stage with other actors (patients, consultants, other doctors). Some of these themes are dealt with further in the questions that follow.

Questions

Self-examination questions

What is meant by the following terms?

- role
- sick role
- 'normalization'
- clinical freedom
- disabled role

- curing
- healing
- bio-medical model
- psycho-social model
- relationship

Essay or discussion questions

1   Answer the question at the end of the passage.

Doctors 'fail to respect nurses'

Nearly half of Britain's nurses are dissatisfied with their relationship with doctors, believing they are still patronised and seen as subordinates rather than as partners, a survey has found.

Despite changes in nurse education and philosophy over recent years, emphasising that they are professionals in their own right, many of the old images of nurses as 'handmaidens' to doctors still exist on the wards, the survey suggests.

The survey of 630 nurses found that almost half the sample felt relationships were better with younger doctors, although this feeling was not universal, with one nurse calling them arrogant.

Asked if they were satisfied with their professional relationship with doctors, 48 per cent of the survey said yes, but 47 per cent said no.

Nearly a third of the sample, when asked how they saw their relationship with doctors, said they were subordinate.

Although 42 per cent said they felt themselves to be in a partnership with doctors, overall 70 per cent of nurses said they felt doctors did not understand nursing work.

Lack of consultation and respect for their opinions were the biggest factors in making nurses unhappy with their relationship with doctors.

One nurse commented of consultants: 'They seem to be frantically trying to keep hold of their authority, while the rest of us, doctors and nurses, are working together for the benefit of patients.'

Two-thirds of nurses felt there was no difference in relationships with female doctors. Where a difference was perceived, female doctors were, on balance, seen as preferable to males.

Half of the sample had been spoken to in an unprofessional manner on occasions by doctors, and for 10 per cent this was a frequent event (from Chris Mihill, *Guardian*, 11 March 1991).

(a) Why do some nurses feel dissatisfied with their relationship with doctors?
(b) How could communications between doctor and nurse be improved?

Suggestions
- Many nurses feel they are not valued.
- There is strong socialization into their respective occupations (medicine and nursing), and this makes it harder for nurses and doctors to communicate. (See chapter 2 for 'professional socialization').
- Project 2000 and the move to an all-graduate profession in nursing may help to improve communication between the main professions in medicine.

2   Using the following extract, suggest ways in which the doctor–patient relationship could be improved.

The doctor–patient relationship (the problem of uncertainty)

Many writers have commented on the extent to which modern medical practice is characterized by uncertainty. As far as many chronic conditions are concerned, their aetiology (the study of the causes of disease) is not well-understood and no explanation is therefore available to convey to patients. Similarly, prognosis cannot be specified with any certainty since the course of the illness and its outcome may be subject to wide variations. One reason why information may not be given to patients is that there is little information to give. However, others have pointed to the fact that this uncertainty is rarely communicated to the patient and even when doctors are certain about the course of a disease or the outcome of treatment information may be withheld. Davis (1963) studied the families of children with poliomyelitis and found that communication of the child's prognosis to the parents was delayed long after the doctor had a clear idea about the level of residual disability. Reviewing this and other evidence Waitzkin and Stoekle (1972) suggest that maintaining uncertainty is one way doctors can retain control over both the patient and the treatment. Failure to inform patients masks the doctor's own uncertainty, maintains patients' beliefs in the efficacy of medicine and limits their role in decision-making (from Scambler 1991: 87).

Suggestions   It seems from the extract that information is power. Perhaps doctors could be encouraged to be less secretive and patients more assertive in seeking information.

3   Read the passage and answer the questions that follow.

Nursing an image

Ever since 'the lady with the lamp' moved silently between beds mopping fevered brows in Scutari Barracks Hospital, nurses have had worries over their image. The cause of their worry is not the usual one. Nurses are good, kind and wonderful. They represent the Victorian ideal of gentle caring femininity brought only slightly up to date. They have even turned the language of compassion – tender loving care – into the jargon of TLC (tender loving care). In this image lies romance, the nurse as pliant handmaid to the handsome doctor.

What irks nurses is that better pay and professional status have not been reflected in changed public perception. They lack the standing to go with the pay. There is some justice in this. All professions suffer from stereotyping; nurses can at least be thankful that their stereotype is inherently attractive. But one cause is nearer home than the media stereotype. Nurses live and work alongside doctors, who are jealous of their status and keen that nurses should continue in their shadow. It is the doctors' tight hold on medicine they should be challenging.

There is no reason why arrangements for the treatment of the sick should require two sharply demarcated and parallel professions, one mainly male, one mainly female. Nurses should work to dissolve the barriers between the two professions, to push across the no-man's-land between them, assuming ever more paramedical skills without having to retrain from the bottom. It is sad comment on the medical service in Britain that only a tiny handful of nurses graduate to general practice. If every private has a field marshal's baton in his pack, the student nurse should be able to aim for the job of brain surgeon (from The Times, 4 April 1991).

(a)   Does the Florence Nightingale image enhance the interests of nurses?
(b)   What signs of improvement can you discern in the nurse's lot? What are the obstacles to improvement?

Suggestions
- The role of nurse is not a high-status one. Discuss the reasons for this.
- Professionalism is sometimes confining. This seems particularly true of the medical profession which emphasizes strict discipline, especially self-discripline.

---

4 What has gone wrong in this case study?

The doctor has just admitted his new patient and requests a trolley to be prepared for lumbar puncture.

He is about to approach the patient with the junior nurse, when staff nurse intervenes: 'I wish you would let me know what you're doing and not just take one of the nurses like this.'

Doctor: 'But I needed the help, and I want to get on with it.'

Staff nurse: 'Well that's OK but does it occur to you that you might have disrupted the care of some other patient by just taking my nurse?'

Doctor: 'Well, my work's more important.'

Staff nurse: 'Anyway, have you asked that patient if you can do the L.P., and have you explained to him what the purposes and outcome might be?'

Doctor: 'I think you should mind your own business.'

Staff nurse: 'I'm not, I'm minding the patient's, please will you talk to the patient first and give him a full explanation, otherwise I'll have to discuss it with your Consultant before the nurses will help you to go ahead doctor.'

The doctor bangs his stethoscope on the trolley and leaves the two nurses. A little later staff nurse chats with the patient and discreetly checks to see if the doctor has, indeed, given a full explanation (he has). The next day, after the Consultant round and during a case conference, the doctor openly challenges the nurse in front of their colleagues. Heated debate ensues with several others joining in (community nurse, health visitor, physiotherapist). In this instance, the Consultant agrees with the nurse (much to her surprise) and the doctor feels isolated (from Wright 1986: 130–1).

Suggestion Nursing is still bureaucratically organized. With a hierarchy, therefore, it is inevitable that nurses will have conflict not only with other professionals but with each other at different levels. Salvage (1985) has noted how often the questioning, assertive nurse is often branded a 'troublemaker' and, in consequence, suffers in career prospects. Nurses who complain to managers (themselves under pressure) about staffing levels may often have their cause seen, not as justified, but as an indictment of themselves. Thus the manager may see the nurse not as someone acting responsibly to preserve standards but as a carping critic who is blameworthy because she cannot cope. The problem is seen as a fault in the individual rather than the system. Openness of ideas and expression in nursing requires the same in management and education. Perhaps there should be an open formal complaints procedure.

Further Reading

See Bibliography for full details.

D. Armstrong, *An Outline of Sociology as Applied to Medicine* (1983b).
E. Freidson (ed.), *Professional Powers* (1986).
E. Goffman, *The Presentation of Self in Everyday Life* (1969).
E. Goffman, *Stigma* (1990).
N. Hart, *The Sociology of Health and Medicine* (1985).
M. Morgan, M. Calnan and N. Manning, *Sociological Approaches to Health and Medicine* (1985).
D. Silverman, *Communication and Medical Practice* (1987).
S. G. Wright, *Building and Using a Model of Nursing* (1986).

5 Inequalities of Health

1 Introduction

Inequalities of health are, like the poor, always with us. Studies of these inequalities highlight the difference between rich and poor, between poverty and affluence, health and illness, the good life and the blighted life, for without good health you are hardly even a full independent citizen of your own country.

It is interesting to look back at the history of these inequalities in order to understand their nature. Wartime Britain fought not only the common enemy but also bad health and poor welfare provisions generally, a legacy of the thirties and before. It may surprise some readers that the Beveridge Report, which demonstrates these inequalities and sets out a programme of welfare, was actually commissioned in 1941, one of the years of greatest peril for Britain. Sometimes war can be a major impetus for welfare, since it unites the nation.

2 The Inequalities of Health

One of the war aims was that every member of the state was to be seen as a full citizen with equal rights with fellow citizens and entitled to full welfare benefits. According to Marshall (1963: 74), these rights contained three parts: *civil*, the right to individual freedom; *political*, the right to participate in the exercise of political power; and *social*, the right to social welfare.

Going back still further, the cry of the soldiers of the First World War was 'homes fit for heroes' after the squalor of the trenches and of their own hovels back home.

At the turn of the century two investigators, Booth and Rowntree, surprised their contemporaries (in London and York respectively) with the amount of poverty they discovered at that time. Another surprise was the number of young men unfit for military service. In 1917 the National Service Medical Board found that only three out of nine conscripts were perfectly fit and healthy (Perkins 1990: 35).

From the 1940s to the 1970s the British welfare state, based on Beveridge's principles, made free medical treatment available to all according to need and regardless of ability to pay. It is this '*universalism*' that is questioned now, mainly on the grounds of cost.

Much of this chapter is concerned with the inequalities of health and the relationship of class and lifestyles to disease, and at the end of the chapter there are exercises designed to help readers apply their knowledge to actual health problems.

The next chapter investigates the more hidden social causes of disease and in particular examines closely the effects of stress.

Two important reports on these issues appeared in the 1980s. First the 1980 Black Report (named after Sir Douglas Black, president of the Royal College of Physicians), published in 1982, demonstrated the inequalities of health – how the worse off got the poorest treatment. Then a report first published by the Health Education Council in 1987, *The Health Divide* (Whitehead 1988), showed that these inequalities were getting bigger. These two reports were later published together as *Inequalities in Health* (Townsend and Davidson 1988).

The Black Report suggests that there has been a turning back from the 'universalistic' approach to welfare to one based more on the market – market demand deciding what the health service should provide and at what price, and individuals being encouraged to choose the service they want.

The problem is that health provision is becoming increasingly expensive. We are living longer, and old people require more medical care. Thus in 1901 the expectation of life at birth of a male baby was 46 years compared with 73 in 1989. The figures for females were 49 and 78 respectively (*Social Trends* (1991), table 7.2). Better care can now be given to the elderly, for example hip replacement joints. In general we are improving techniques such as organ transplants and heart-bypass operations. Table 5.1 shows this increase in demand.

Table 5.1   UK National Health Service hospital in-patient waiting lists, by speciality (thousands)

	1976	1991
General surgery	200.5[a]	169.0
Orthopaedics	109.8	151.5
Ear, nose or throat	121.7	125.3
Gynaecology	91.8	97.8
Oral surgery	26.5	49.7
Plastic surgery	44.7	41.7
Ophthalmology	41.2	99.5
Urology	22.0[b]	46.7
Other	42.5	49.0
All specialities	700.8	830.1

[a]Includes the Northern Ireland figures for 'Urology'.
[b]Great Britain only.
Source: Adapted from *Social Trends* (1992), p. 138, table 7.33. Calculated from Department of Health, Welsh Office, Scottish Health Service, Common Services Agency, Department of Health and Social Services, Northern Ireland

3   Health and Social Class

Social class is used as a category in these reports and also throughout this book. It is based on the occupation of heads of household. According to the classification used by the Registrar General, the categories are as follows (percentages are given for each group):

I   Professional (for example, accountant, doctor, lawyer) (5 per cent)

II   Intermediate (for example, manager, nurse, schoolteacher) (18 per cent)

IIIN   Skilled non-manual (for example, clerical worker, secretary, shop assistant) (12 per cent)

IIIM   Skilled manual (for example, bus driver, butcher, carpenter, coal-face worker) (38 per cent)

IV   Partly skilled (for example, agricultural worker, bus conductor, postman) (18 per cent)

V   Unskilled (for example, cleaner, dock worker, labourer) (9 per cent)

It should be mentioned that there are several other ways of measuring class, as will be seen from the tables quoted later. Some sociologists such as Josephine Klein prefer to use the concept of lifestyles when trying to classify people and events.

Tables 5.2 to 5.9 tell us about the relative positions of people in different social classes and their health. Table 5.2 shows that people employed in manual occupations have a higher mortality ratio than those employed in non-manual occupations. (If the standard mortality ratio (SMR) of a sub-group were 100 it would mean that people in that sub-group would have an equal chance of dying as the group as a whole.)

Table 5.2 Standard mortality ratios[a] for select causes of death in Great Britain, 1979–1983, among men aged 20–54 and 55–64

Cause of death	Age	Non-manual classes	Manual classes
All causes	20–54	76	115
	55–64	82	117
	20–64	80	116
Lung cancer	20–54	60	133
	55–64	67	128
	20–64	65	129
Coronary heart disease	20–54	80	113
	55–64	90	117
	20–64	87	114
Cerebro-vascular disease	20–54	73	121
	55–64	77	119
	20–64	76	120

[a]For each cause, and within each age-group, the standard mortality ratio (SMR) for all men in 1979–1983 is 100.
Source: Reproduced in Townsend and Davidson (1982: 231)

Table 5.3 uses infant mortality as its measure. Here the number of deaths per 1000 births is used. There is a big difference in infant mortality rates between classes I and II and classes IV and V. Despite the general drop in infant mortality rates between 1975 and 1983, the differences between classes remain wide.

Not only are the big differences in mortality ratios between classes. There are also big differences between races, as table 5.4 shows. Why do these ethnic differences occur? Is it because there are physical differences between races that makes them susceptible to one disease but not another? In a well-known study, Gordon (1957, 1967) demonstrated the very large differences between the USA and Japan in the incidence of coronary heart disease. Japan has one of the lowest rates of the disease, while the USA has one of the highest. However, Japanese people living in America have a similar rate of the disease as do Americans. In Hawaii, which is halfway between the USA and Japan, the rates for Japanese are halfway between US and Japanese rates.

What is the significance of these findings? It seems that health, class behaviour, lifestyles and mortality may not be due primarily to what we have inherited from our parents physically and mentally. Rather our health and lifestyles may be due to what we have learnt from earliest childhood and from our later contact with the social world generally.

Returning to the main theme of this section, health and social class, the editors of *The Health Divide* felt that poorer people damaged their health more through smoking and drinking but that the health gap would be wide without this anyway. The editors concluded that real improvements in social and working conditions are necessary for this gap to be closed (Townsend and Davidson 1988: 304–5). The gap is substantial, whether measured by class, income, car ownership or housing provision, and it is general so that, for example, all major killer diseases affect the poor more than the rich. People in the less-

Table 5.3 Infant mortality by occupational class, 1975–1984

Perinatal deaths per 1000 total births	1975	1984
Rate for classes I and II	15.0	7.7
Rate for classes IV and V	22.7	12.3

Source: Derived from OPCS data, series DH3, various years; reproduced in Townsend and Davidson (1982: 259)

Table 5.4 Summary of main findings of Immigrant Mortality Study, England and Wales, 1970–1978

Mortality by cause	Comparison with death rates for England and Wales
Tuberculosis	High in immigrants from the Indian sub-continent, Ireland, the Caribbean, Africa and Scotland
Liver cancer	High in immigrants from the Indian sub-continent, the Caribbean and Africa
Cancer of stomach, large intestine, breast	Low mortality among Indians
Ischaemic heart disease	High mortality found in immigrants from the Indian sub-continent
Hypertension and stroke	Strikingly high mortality among immigrants from the Caribbean and Africa – four to six times higher for hypertension and twice as high for strokes as the level in England and Wales
Diabetes	High among immigrants born in the Caribbean and the Indian sub-continent
Obstructive lung disease (including chronic bronchitis)	Low in all immigrants in comparison with ratio for England and Wales
Maternal mortality	High in immigrants from Africa, the Caribbean, and to a lesser extent the Indian sub-continent
Violence and accidents	High in all immigrant groups

Source: Adapted from Marmot et al. (1984)

favoured occupations have higher sickness rates and the children of these workers also experience higher sickness, lower birth rates and shorter stature. Women have lower death rates than men, but experience higher sickness rates than men. (See chapter 8 for a discussion of women and health.) There are big regional and ethnic differences.

Readers may feel that the book *Inequalities of Health* has demon-strated that the inequalities do in fact exist and that we should do something about it if we want a healthier population. Ivan Reid in *Social Class Differences* has highlighted these inequalities still further (Reid 1989). Tables 5.5 to 5.9 demonstrate inequalities in illness, care of sight, hearing and teeth, smoking, drinking and eating, and obesity.

4   Propositions Relating to the Inequalities of Health

Proposition 1

Sociologists rely too heavily on the concept of class in analysing problems such as the relationship between social class and disease.

The fact is that class is still with us, and this is perhaps demonstrated clearly in the various tables quoted in this chapter. Thus there is a

Table 5.5 Self-reported health and health behaviour, by social class and sex (percentages)

	Social class 1[a]	Social class 6[a]	Male	Female	All
Chronic sickness	20	38	29	31	30
Limiting chronic sickness	9	27	16	18	17
Acute sickness	11	15	11	14	13
Number of restricted-activity days in 12 months					
Men	13	25			20
Women	20	44			29
Consulted NHS GP in 14 days prior to interview	11	18	11	16	14

[a]Social class 1 corresponds to class I in the Registrar General's system and social class 6 corresponds to class V.
Source: Adapted from Reid (1989: 131). Devised from tables 8.19, 8.20, 8.24 and 8.26, *General Household Survey* (1985); table 7.5 *GHS* (1980); table 6.38, *GSH* (1984); and table 2.14, *Health and Lifestyle Survey* (1987)

Table 5.6 Sight, hearing and teeth, by social class and sex (percentages)

	Social class 1	Social class 6	Male	Female	All
Sight					
Wears glasses	67	57	57	67	62
Had difficulty	10	19	12	16	14
Hearing					
Wears hearing aid, or has difficulty	7	21	15	12	13
Teeth					
No natural teeth	6	39	20	27	23
Regular check-up with dentist	68	30	42	58	50

Source: Adapted from Reid (1989: 135). Devised from tables 8.35 and 8.37, *General Household Survey* (1982); tables 7.19 and 7.20, *GHS* (1979); and tables 8.34, 8.35, 8.38 and 8.39, *GHS* (1985).

Table 5.7 Cigarette smoking,[a] by social class and sex

	Social class 1	Social class 6	Men	Women	All
Percentages					
Current smokers	16	42	36	32	34
Ex-regular smokers	28	18	30	17	23
Never/occasional smokers	56	40	34	51	44
Average number of cigarettes smoked per week per smoker					
Men	108	114			115
Women	78	96			96

[a]By persons aged over 16 years.
Source: Adapted from Reid (1989: 144). Devised from tables 10.6 and 10.7, *General Household Survey* (1984).

relationship between social class and disease, but these distinctions penetrate our everyday social life such as care of our eyesight, hearing, teeth, our habits in eating and drinking (especially alcohol). Class is a useful tool for analysing all these items – but not the only tool.

Table 5.8   Adult alcohol-drinking habits, by social class and sex (percentages)

	Social class 1	Social class 6	Men	Women	All
Heavy[a]	5	12	20	2	10
Moderate[b]	8	8	14	4	9
Light[c]	73	41	50	61	56
Occasional[d]	8	20	9	20	15
Abstainer	7	18	7	13	10

[a]Drinks 7 or more units (e.g. half a pint beer/measure of spirit/glass of wine) between once a week and most days.
[b]Drinks 7 or more units once/twice a month or 5–6 units between once a week and most days.
[c]Drinks 1–4 units between once a month and most days.
[d]Drinks 1 or more units between once a year and twice in 6 months.
Note. Since drinking was based on type of drink most regularly used, it may underestimate drinking of those who use more than one type.
Source: Adapted from Reid (1989: 145). Calculated from table 11.4, *General Household Survey* (1984)

Table 5.9   Obese adults,[a] by sex and social class of head of household (percentages)

	Social class						
	1	2	3	4	5	6	All
Men	5	10	6	9	7	13	8
Women	6	13	12	18	17	19	15

[a]Based on Body Mass Index (BMI) derived from weight (kilos) over height (metres) squared; and defined, for men, BMI = 30.0 and over, for women, BMI = 28.6 and over.
Source: Reid (1989: 143). Calculated from table 4.7, *The Health and Lifestyle Survey* (1987)

Proposition 2

Inequalities are not necessarily a bad thing. They encourage effort.

It is sometimes suggested that inequality in a society is not necessarily a bad thing; it may be a spur to action. Segalman and Marsland (1989) stress the need for competition and individualism in society to bring out the best in people rather than allowing them to live off the state. Thus people at the bottom of the social scale have an incentive to better themselves when they see others enjoying a higher standard of living. The trouble here is that, although there is some social mobility in society, most people do not rise much in the social scale.

In this chapter and the next it is shown that inequality leads to worse health and that if there were less inequality (of income, housing, etc.) there might be better health. If those at the bottom of the social scale had the same income, living conditions, and so on, as those at the top, much ill-health might disappear. This does not require a miracle cure, only a fairer society. The facts set out in this chapter would seem to support this view, but do you agree with the proposition expressed in the two sentences above?

Proposition 3

Most people would prefer private medicine if they could afford it. We should allow market forces (supply and demand) to say what should be produced at what price.

Table 5.10 shows a big increase in the use and availability of services provided by the private nursing sector in England and Wales. It may seem a good idea to allow the free market to operate in these matters – but there are some consequences to be considered.

First, 'leaving it to the market' implies that the government need do nothing, that producers and consumers should fix the price between themselves. But really the negotiations are uneven. The consumers of welfare include the very old, the infirm, the sick, and the inhabitants of 'Cardboard City'. The government cannot allow all these people in need just to drop out (or drop dead, literally).

Table 5.10 Private health services, England and Wales

	1971	1986
Registered nursing homes and private hospitals:		
beds available (thousands)	25.3	65.1
Private out-patient attendances (thousands)	87.0	261.6

Source: Department of Health; Welsh Office; reproduced in *Social Trends* (1991)

Proposition 4

A lot of ill-health is due to bad diet. The poor do not eat wisely. Perhaps the government should persuade people to eat healthier food – more fibre and less fat.

The weakness of this proposition is that the sociologist sees diet as more than just a list of food items. Rather, diet (which includes eating, drinking and smoking) is part of a way of life which includes injudicious spending. Note, for example, that poor people are more likely to carry on smoking despite the anti-smoking propaganda (see also pp. 65–6 for the idea of 'the splash'). Here we are perhaps dealing with lifestyles rather than just class.

Proposition 5

Many claimants for welfare benefits do not want to work. They do not take care of their own health – they smoke and drink – and they do not look after the family's health.

This line of argument has an ancient ancestry. It can be traced back to Tudor times, when 'scroungers' were known as 'sturdy beggars'. In later times the Victorians made the distinction between the deserving poor, who were given help, and the undeserving poor, who could be sent to the workhouse to work for their living. Being sent to the workhouse was a disgrace which lingered long after the old Poor Law was abolished. However, many poor people can be destitute through no fault of their own. They may be unemployed or become ill. When the Beveridge reforms were implemented in the 1940s we seem to have had a strong sense of community.

There are some other terms which sociologists have used: (a) *underclass*, implying its members are not really part of the main society; (b) *reserve army of the unemployed*, referring to people who are employed when business is good and laid off when it is bad; (c) *dualism in the labour market* – there is one labour market for good jobs and another for poor jobs and the markets do not meet.

Proposition 6

The welfare state protects the poorest. It provides a safety net below which they cannot fall. This has been the intention behind much welfare legislation.

This would seem to be a reasonable proposition, yet Titmuss (1976) questions it. Certainly one of the aims of the Beveridge Report, published in 1942, had been to achieve greater equality between rich and poor. But there has not been much evidence for a transfer of income from rich to poor. Table 5.11 shows that inequality of income has increased substantially. Thus it will be seen that in 1976–7 the top 1 per cent of taxpayers had 11 per cent of income, and by 1990–1 their share had increased to 14 per cent. Note the corresponding gap for the bottom 50 per cent.

The gap between rich and poor remains wide for many reasons. The poor do not always apply for what they are entitled to. The wealthy are more likely to know their rights. In particular, students in higher and further education are much more likely to be the children of the well-to-do.

Table 5.11 Shares of total income tax liability (percentages)

	1976–7	1990–1
Top 1 per cent of taxpayers	11	14
Lowest 50 per cent of taxpayers	20	15

Source: Inland Revenue and *Social Trends* (1991)

5 Concluding Questions

Why do inequalities of health persist?

Inequalities of health may be a reflection of inequalities in society as a whole. It is probable that one cannot substantially improve the health of society without removing some of these obvious inequalities. Again the disadvantages suffered by poorer people seem to be passed on to the next generation, and these include poor diet, poor housing, poor working conditions and poor education. The concept of social-ization, discussed in chapter 2, is important here. Children are socialized for their place in society (as is the nurse). Children see their parents under stress due to the disadvantages mentioned here, and thus they then learn that their parents' behaviour is normal – this is the reality they come to accept and pass on to the next generation. In this way parents are agents of society; they ensure society reproduces itself.

What can be done about inequalities of health?

More emphasis on sociology in the curriculum for nurses and others may help to show how society really works. Ask yourself whether a 'fairer' society (one with fewer inequalities of wealth) would be a healthier society. Should government encourage people to be more independent and make their own medical arrangements? Some of the work set later in this chapter tackles these questions.

What can the nurse do?

Again, the nurse should be aware of the nature of the social world. In particular she or he should be aware that it is the medical profession that applies the medical model. The medical model treats the body as a machine in which a part needs repair. It fails to treat the whole body or the whole person, or the whole person in his or her social world (see Kennedy 1981).

Finally it should be clearly recognized that poor health comes in large part from poor social conditions and stress, as this chapter and the next show. It is the source of illness that must be identified; 'patching' people up will not solve the problem of ill-health if the source is not identified.

Questions

Self-examination questions

What is meant by the following?

- inequalities of health
- Beveridge Report
- citizen
- universalism
- individualism

- free market
- social class
- standard mortality ratio
- infant mortality ratio
- 'Cardboard City'

Essay or discussion questions

1 What are the advantages and disadvantages of using social class as a measure of health and attitudes?
 Suggestion You could use income bands, or type of house or car. Class is a useful measure because it indicates a way of life, including standard of living, diet, health habits, etc. Some sociologists (e.g. M. Weber, M. Blaxter and J. Klein) have used lifestyles to classify society.

2 Discuss the view that class is still with us.
 Suggestion In addition to the readings used here, see also Blaxter (1990).

3 Read the following passage and answer these questions.
(a) What is meant by 'the splash'?
(b) Does the concept of 'the splash' still exist?
(c) How would you relate this passage to the rest of the chapter.

The splash

There are occasions when the whole extended family makes an effort to meet. In Mrs. Shipway's family, this was as often as every week. Normally, it would be at least on each birthday, with something special on Mum's birthday, at Christmas, and weddings.

Good cheer and an air of festivity accompany these family occasions.

The deep feeling for home, the emotional significance of which seems to surpass all others, makes it congenial that there should every now and then be a joyous affirmation of the unity of the family in the home. The 'splash' is a rite in the religion of the family. But the need for an occasional outburst of this kind is also deeply rooted in the life-situation and personality-structure of this population. The splash is a short-term equivalent of the indulgence which marks certain age-groups, such as infancy and adolescence: the immediate gratification of impulses is a necessary counterpoise to the more rigorous conditions which obtain at other times and is justified by reference to the general harshness of life. 'Gather ye rosebuds while ye may' can be taken to refer not only to age-groups but more generally to the rhythm of a life which is usually harsh and demanding but which allows well-defined occasions when the demands may legitimately be ignored and the rosebuds gathered (from Klein 1965: 193–4).

Suggestions   Mention that people seldom change their diet in the long term. Therefore eating, drinking and smoking patterns continue even though the family may have hit bad times through poor health, say, or unemployment. Thus, for example, Friday night may continue to be party night. Heavy smoking and drinking may not be so reprehensible when considered against the backgrounds of the drinking of much working-class life and leisure.

---

4   How would you justify the freedom of the market place in health care, with patients paying for their own health care?
    Suggestions   You may find useful the book by Segalman and Marsland (1989), which emphasizes that people should be independent and not rely on 'welfare handouts'. See also Titmuss (1976), for a contrary view.

---

5   As a sociologist, what in the following report would you wish to investigate further and what methods of social investigation would you wish to use? See chapter 9 for methods of research.

'Damning' report on health of Aborigines

Australia's native Aborigines die some 20 years younger than the average white Australians and have more than double the rate of heart disease, a 'damning' health study has shown.

Canberra's Australian Institute of Health reports in tomorrow's issue of the Medical Journal of Australia, that Aboriginal males have – depending where they live – a life expectancy of between 53 and 61 years. Aboriginal women range from 58 to 65 years.

This compares with the life expectancy for other Australians of 73 years for men and 79 years for women. Aborigines make up 1.4 per cent of Australia's 17 million population.

Dr Neil Thomson of the institute said in Canberra that while infant mortality had improved, the life opportunity for Aborigines was 'quite dismal'. 'The whole thing is incredibly damning,' he added.

His report added that Aboriginal deaths from circulatory diseases are on average 2.4 times higher than for whites, and from respiratory ailments some 6.7 times higher.

Deaths from car accidents, falls, drownings and homicides were 3.5 to 4.3 times higher than for whites.

The report adds that there are a disproportionate number of Aboriginal deaths in the 25- to 44-year-old age group.

'You would have to go back to the turn of the century to find life expectancies this low [among white Australians],' Dr Thomson said (from Dr N. Thomson, *Observer*, 17 February 1991).

---

6 Read the extract and tables from Blaxter (1990) and answer the questions that follow.

Exercise is defined solely as leisure-time physical activity. It is generally agreed that this is what is relevant to health, especially for protection against coronary heart disease, and activity which is undertaken as part of work is a matter which has to be considered separately. Respondents to the survey were asked in detail about the sporting and other energetic activities, including keep-fit activities, which they had done, 'in the last fortnight', and also about the time spent in leisure-time walking and gardening. The scale used in the table is derived from calculations of energy expended in all these activities. The possibility arises, of course, that 'the last fortnight' may not represent a typical period for some individual respondents. However, the patterns of activity which resulted appeared to have a good face validity, and this form of questioning was thought preferable to more general and less quantifiable descriptions.

Leisure-time physical activity is, of course, strongly related to age. Among men under 40, 17 per cent claimed to have done some running or jogging in 'the last fortnight', and 20 per cent of women of the same age said that they had engaged in some keep-fit activity. Only 3 per cent of women over 60 did so. The more active sporting pursuits and keep-fit activities were also, among those under 60, much more likely to be part of the lifestyle of those with higher educational qualifications and those in non-manual rather than manual households. For instance, among those aged 18–40 years, 42 per cent (male) and 51 per cent (female) in manual households said that they took part in no sporting or keep-fit activities at all, although they might have done some walking or gardening, compared with 30 per cent (male) and 38 per cent (female) in non-manual households. This pattern of participation matches well with that which has been reported in other surveys for the British population (e.g. General Household Survey 1978) (from Blaxter 1990: 120–1).

(a) How would you account for the differences between men and women, manual and non-manual workers, and older and younger workers, in exercise patterns?
(b) Is exercise good for you?
(c) What (if anything) should the government do?
(d) How might the views of a nurse differ from those of a sociologist?

Suggestions
● Many women seem to give up sport when they marry. What can be done about this?
● The sociologist might see the high-status people doing most of the sport, e.g. non-manual rather than manual workers, men rather than women, and so on.

Table: Distribution of exercise categories, per cent, comparing non-manual and manual social classes

Category	Age 18–39		40–59		60+	
	Non-man.	Man.	Non-man.	Man.	Non-man.	Man.
Males						
1. High level of vigorous exercise.	25	22	14	9	7	4
2. Moderate level of vigorous exercise.	23	18	15	10	6	6
3. Some vigorous exercise.	17	11	10	9	7	6
4. Some exercise but no sport, keep-fit etc.	9	13	16	15	17	19
5. Little exercise.	9	13	21	29	31	27
6. No exercise.	17	22	25	28	32	36
(N = 100%)	(673)	(953)	(516)	(724)	(362)	(630)
Females						
1. High level of vigorous exercise.	14	9	9	7	3	2
2. Moderate level of vigorous exercise.	21	15	13	10	4	7
3. Some vigorous exercise.	19	16	16	12	7	4
4. Some exercise but no sport, keep-fit etc.	13	16	13	13	12	13
5. Little exercise.	15	21	21	26	27	24
6. No exercise.	19	23	29	33	47	51
(N = 100%)	(994)	(1,119)	(727)	(852)	(515)	(806)

Further Reading

See Bibliography for full details.

M. Blaxter, *Health and Lifestyles* (1990).
K. Jones, J. Brown and J. Bradshaw, *Issues in Social Policy* (1983).
I. Reid, *Social Class Differences in Britain* (1989).
G. Scambler (ed.), *Sociology as Applied to Medicine* (1991).
R. Segalman and D. Marsland, *From Cradle to Grave* (1989).
R. Titmuss, *Essays on 'The Welfare State'* (1976).
P. Townsend and N. Davidson (eds), *Inequalities in Health* (1988).

6 What Makes Us Ill?

1 Introduction

In the previous chapter it was demonstrated that there was a close connection between social class and disease and premature death.

For example, cigarette smoking is related to class; it is also related to lung cancer and heart disease. But smoking and class can be measured. What is much more difficult to measure is the underlying stress which seems to have caused this smoking in the first place. Indeed, *is* there stress in the first place? Might not some smoking be due to the cult of masculinity, for example? How, then, would you explain the number of female smokers?

Mitchell (1984) asks what makes us ill. We know little about the effect of the environment on disease, and, in order to help us measure stress, she suggests eight dimensions affecting illness and health.

What makes us ill? What keeps us well? Readers are encouraged to tackle the projects and other problems suggested and to develop their own insights into these questions.

Sociological knowledge can be used to investigate possible social causes of illness, since sociology as a discipline studies the effects of society upon its individual members (see Durkheim (1952) whose work is quoted later in this chapter). This chapter offers some examples of the social causes and effects of illness including suicide, drug-taking, accidents and stress generally. Finally the chapter discusses the social construction of illness, asking to what extent are illnesses of our own making?

2 The Nature of Stress and Illness

Mitchell (1984) asks, in her first chapter: who gets ill? In reply she says there are two myths about illness: the first is that it strikes at random; the second is that in these days it is diseases of affluence that are the problem – the wealthy man who has a heart attack, for instance. She then quotes a number of case studies which confirm that these are myths, including a study by Rose and Marmot (1981) which recorded deaths from heart attacks among male civil servants who worked in Whitehall. The following facts emerged from these studies.

First, over a seven-year period more than a thousand had died, almost a half from heart attacks. Among the 960 civil servants on the top grades there were only nine deaths. Among the 1625 men on the bottom grades eighty-seven died. Among the senior civil servants the death rate was less than one in a hundred. Among the civil servants doing unskilled work the death rate was more than one in twenty.

Mitchell argues that our health is as intimately linked with the conditions of our work as it was a century ago. As for diseases of affluence, there is clearly something wrong with the idea that heart attacks are an 'executive's condition', since the evidence shows it is the poor who get the most heart attacks.

Mitchell believes that, because we tend to think of illness coming from germs or coming out of the blue, we overlook the ways in which health reflects our environment. Yet, says Mitchell, many common 'killer' diseases are less of a mystery than we think. We now know a lot about the causes of strokes and heart disease, but even cancer can to some extent be seen as a product of our environment. Cancer can be caused by a number of carcinogens (or cancer agents) including asbestos, tobacco, certain food additives, pollution, industrial dusts and poor housing conditions (the politics of cancer are discussed towards the end of this chapter).

The theme of Mitchell's book is that there is a strong connection between social conditions and disease, and she suggests that, in thinking about what damages our health and what keeps us well, eight key dimensions emerge. These dimensions are based on interviews with people who live and work in bad conditions, and they are as follows.

Eight dimensions of stress

1 How much we are exposed to a hazardous environment, both inside and outside of work. . . .

2 How exhausted our work inside and outside the home makes us (due perhaps to excessive overtime) and how much time and space we have for recuperation. . . .

3 How much money we take home. Overtime, bonus schemes and the rest may be exhausting, but they are often the only way to make enough money to live on. Earnings are crucial. Of all the factors in the Whitehall study, income proved a much more powerful predictor of whether a man got heart disease than all the physiological measures, including blood plasma cholesterol and blood pressure.

4 How many worries we have and how deep and sustained they are. Including worries about work, about losing your job. . . .

5 How hopeful or helpless we feel. How hopeful we feel for the future affects how much we are prepared to invest in our own health now.

6 How powerless or powerful we feel. We need power in controlling our lives. . . .

7 How bored or alienated we feel. George and Baden [two interviewees on Mitchell's survey] describe how destructive monotonous work can be, and how not feeling in control of what you are making, whether it is a tractor or a machine tool, leaves a hollow feeling.

8 How lonely or loved we feel. The loss of someone close to you . . . has long been recognized as having consequences for our health. Spouses often die within a short period of one another. Loss is a major factor in depression and in increasing vulnerability to illness. Equally, having someone

to talk to and share feelings with can make us less likely
to become ill. But it is not just very intimate and family
relationships which affect us; so does having workmates and
neighbours to be friends with. Vera contrasts the isolation
of the tower block with the friendliness of the old neighbour-
hoods. (Mitchell 1984: 107–11)

What can medicine do to improve the health of poor people?

People bring their medical problems to the doctor: ulcers, bronchitis,
depression. But the doctor is trying to cope with a high workload.
Doctors have to admit they have no cures for many of the problems
they face (Mitchell 1984: 17–18). Sometimes it is assumed that people
are the problem, yet those we used to call 'feckless' we might now
call deprived. The patient may be told: you should come off the pill,
stop smoking or overeating, or change your job. On leaving hospital
patients are often no healthier, but they come home to the same
situation in which they became ill. In all this it seems doctors seldom
tackle the question why this group of people became ill and not the
other group, as professionals tend to discuss problems with fellow
professionals.

3   Social Causes of Disease

What, then, are the social causes of disease and how can a sociologist
highlight them? This section describes some social causes of disease,
although in our present state of knowledge we cannot, of course,
fully explain them. For example, Fitzpatrick (1982) argues there are
not two kinds of disease, psychological and non-psychological. Rather,
psychological stress may have produced vulnerability to a wide range
of disease from colds to cancer.

Bereavement is a devastating form of stress. Parkes et al. (1969)
in a study of widowers aged fifty-five and over found an increase in

mortality, largely from cardiovascular disease, for six months after their bereavement.

Work can be another source of stress, though often it is not the work itself but rather change or increased pressure. Thus Timio and Gentili (1976) showed that when workers moved from normal payment to piecework there was a large increase in stress.

Friedman and Rosenman (1974) showed that what they called a type-A person was more liable to heart attack than type B. Type-A behaviour is characterized by extreme competitiveness, aggressiveness and a sense of pressure of time.

Life events can be stressful, as table 6.1 shows. (It uses a scale according to which respondents' replies are scored.)

Table 6.2 contains a summary of case studies showing that bad health is associated with bad social conditions.

Table 6.1 Some examples of values of life events on the social readjustment rating scale

Death of spouse	100
Divorce	73
Marriage	50
Major change in responsibilities at work	29
Changes in residence	20
Vacation	13

Source: Adapted from Patrick and Scambler (1986)

4 Further Sociological Insights into Illness and Health

Sociology seems to be able to shed some light on the social causes of ill-health. Here now are a few more sociological insights into possible causes of ill-health.

Suicide

Sociologists have shown that there is a relationship between suicide and social facts. Thus Durkheim (1952), one of the 'founding fathers'

Table 6.2   Deprivation and ill-health: small-area analyses

Areas studied	Findings
37 municipal wards in Glasgow, 23 wards in Edinburgh	Clear evidence of greater mortality and morbidity in areas of greater deprivation (except for perinatal and infant deaths)
29 wards in Sheffield	Clear correlation between 'areas of poverty' and mortality for men and women. For men, life expectancy over eight years greater in most affluent wards compared with most deprived.
28 wards in Bristol	Poor health significantly correlated with deprivation.
755 wards in London	Mortality rates in the most deprived wards nearly double those of the least deprived wards.
678 wards in Northern region	Correspondence between ill-health and deprivation extremely close. The strongest association between health and deprivation variables was with lack of a car (proxy for low income).
36 geographic clusters of wards in England and Wales. Longitudinal study. Individuals linked directly with data.	Pattern of low mortality in high-status clusters and high mortality in low-status clusters.

Source: Whitehead (1988: 249)

of modern sociology, demonstrated that those who had a strong sense of belonging to a community were less likely to commit suicide. Hence he showed that Catholics were less likely to commit suicide than Protestants, married people less than single, country inhabitants less than town dwellers, and so on. The main rules of his sociological method of investigation are summarized as follows: there are social facts such as groups, etc.; social facts are external to individuals yet constrain their behaviour; the researcher should measure *rates* of behaviour, for example rates of suicide, with rates of attachment to the group; you cannot give a psychological explanation for sociological behaviour.

In his study of suicide Durkheim identified three kinds of suicide:

(a) Egoistic suicide, which reflects an individualistic ethos in which individuals are responsible for their own salvation.

(b) Anomic suicide, where individuals experience a state of normlessness – where norms clash or are absent. Here individuals are on their own and feel isolated from society. (See also chapter 1 and Glossary for a definition of *norms*.) Imagine also a traditional society whose culture has been crushed with the coming of industrialization.

(c) Altruistic suicide in which individuals glorify the group through their action, for example Japanese fighter pilots in the Second World War who crashed their planes on to American warships. There is also 'fatalism', which consists of an excess of regulation of the person.

Official statistics are often inaccurate. Suicides are more accurately recorded in towns. Highly integrated groups, such as Catholics are more likely to conceal suicides, perhaps because it is regarded as shameful in such groups. Sociologists should always be sceptical of even the most 'elegant' theories.

With high rates of unemployment there have been studies linking unemployment with increased rates of suicide. Thus Platt and Kreitman (1984) have sought to demonstrate a link between male unemployment and attempted suicide, as table 6.3 shows.

Table 6.3 Male unemployment and the risk of suicide

Duration of unemployment	Ratio of risk of attempted suicide of the unemployed to the employed
Less than 6 months	6.1
6–12 months	10.1
Over 12 months	19.1

Source: Adapted from Platt and Kreitman (1984)

Drug-taking

Why include this topic in a chapter entitled 'What Makes Us Ill?'? Because it shows how people do apparently 'dangerous' things, do not change their injurious habits, do not take advice, though individuals get the support of their groups for what they are doing. A leading sociologist in this area is Howard Becker, who wanted to know what made people smoke marijuana. Becker (1963) conducted interviews with fifty users. He showed that, to become a user of the drug, individuals must pass through a number of stages: they must learn to smoke the drug, recognize its effects and learn to enjoy its sensations. In this process individuals develop the motivation to use marijuana. They have learnt to answer yes to the question 'Is it fun?' Once the individual has learnt to enjoy it he or she will continue to use the drug so long as the enjoyment from it continues.

A *group* of drug takers may be seen as a deviant subculture. They have norms and values which are different from those of society as a whole. To the insider (the drug user), it is the outside society that is deviant. The concept of a deviant subculture is very important in sociology. It applies in the sociology of deviance; the sociology of religion; and urban sociology (street gangs) and so on.

Becker concludes that the individual will feel free to use marijuana to the degree that he or she will come to regard the conventional views of the world as the uninformed views of outsiders and replaces them with the inside view that he or she has acquired through experience with the drug in the company of other users (or insiders).

Two further questions arise here. First, should marijuana be decriminalized? Secondly, in what way does the group support the individual member?

It is suggested that marijuana can become addictive and can lead on to taking hard drugs. Thus it can be injurious to health. Becker shows here why, in spite of its danger to health, people continue to smoke it. In answer to the second question, the group and its members all have the same values and this gives them material support even when everyone outside the group has opposite values.

Other examples of taking risks with your health

It seems therefore that many people take risks with their health. The previous chapter described injudicious spending on smoking and alcohol; the concept of the 'splash' is a facet of diet. People eat what they are used to, often without asking whether it is good for them.

Over-eating and lack of exercise are common and are habit-forming. On the other hand, health clubs are for groups of people who want to lose weight and it is interesting to see that these people join weight-reducing *clubs* or groups, perhaps it is easier to lose weight when you have the support of the group.

Preventable disease

One theme of this chapter and the last has been our comparative inability to explain the persistence of killer diseases like heart disease, strokes and cancer.

Epstein (1990) argues that cancer is preventable and that there are vested interests which prevent the true facts about cancer from being known. Governments have a poor record in this regard. Medical schools should reorient their educational programmes from the treatment of cancer to its prevention. Chemicals at home and in the workplace must be clearly labelled. We should be prepared to change our lifestyle, for example by giving up smoking.

'The major determinants of preventable cancer are political and economic, rather than scientific, and as such must be addressed in the open political arena. Cancer prevention must become a major election issue, on a par with inflation' (Epstein 1990).

Two questions could be asked here. First, why has the struggle against cancer been portrayed as mainly a political one? Secondly, what special contribution can sociology make to this debate?

In reply it is suggested that the sociology student should recognize when a political argument is being put up – for example, when it is argued that the 'nation' cannot afford the cost (of cancer prevention, say). Really the nation can afford almost anything, if it is resolved to do so. Consider a nation at war – it will pay anything, make any sacrifice. Another argument is that there are many other important causes that need the money, besides you. This is playing one group against another. A variant is: you are pushing in front of the queue. Cancer prevention costs money – that is to say higher taxes – and this is not popular, hence the political debate about cancer.

5 A Social Construction of Illness

This section begins by examining how disease is perceived by describing some case studies.

Blaxter and Paterson (1982), in a three-generational study of mothers and daughters and of their attitudes to health, found that different groups defined health differently. For the worse-off, health was defined functionally; for example, 'Are you fit for work?' 'Are you fit for your normal role?' On this basis people made a distinction between normal illness and serious illness. Health was 'good'. It implied: carry on – business as usual. Illness was a spiritual or moral malaise, with people saying they were healthy when they were not.

Calman and Johnson (1985) found that people distinguished between diseases they feared getting and those they felt most vulnerable to. Thus many feared they would get cancer, but did not feel personally vulnerable to it; for example, 'Well, I fear getting it but I do not believe I will get it.' Another respondent said: 'I do worry about getting cancer simply because there is so much of it in my family. And I do think every time I get anything I wonder if it is cancer, I must admit I do worry about it' (Calman and Johnson 1985).

The authors conclude that people use their personal experience to make sense of health and illness. This is important for health education campaigners, many of whom use an epidemiological model of disease, judging its distribution and spread. They emphasize reducing risk factors, for example discouraging cigarette smoking. But it is important to emphasize that this was not the model used by the respondents in this case study, as the evidence shows.

It is interesting to take the social construction of illness further. Thus Armstrong (1983b) argues that because all knowledge of the natural world emerges from within a social context that knowledge will be special to the society from which it arose. Thus Darwin's theory of evolution arises from Victorian society with its emphasis on competition.

In order to discuss the social construction of illness it may be useful to consider the 'parent' theory, 'the social construction of reality' (Berger and Luckman 1984) (see also Glossary). According to this theory, people construct a personal view of their social world. This personal view of the world then becomes objectified into an objective view of the world. It becomes a regular pattern of behaviour.

Kennedy (1981) shows how the medical profession can impose its theory of health and disease. 'What is an illness?' he asks. 'The American Psychiatric Association took a vote and decided that homosexuality was not an illness. How extraordinary, you may think, to decide what illness is by taking a vote. What exactly is going on here?' (Kennedy 1981: 1). Kennedy believes medicine has taken the wrong path. An inappropriate form of medicine has been created, largely by doctors (Kennedy 1981: 26). But the nature of modern medicine is positively deleterious to health. We have all been willing participants in allowing the creation of a myth because we like to believe that illness can be cured and death postponed by modern medicine. The myth also seems to serve the interest of the doctors, who could then be seen as miracle workers.

Kennedy (1981: 78) goes on to say that doctors make decisions as to what ought to be done but only some of these decisions are technical decisions. The majority of decisions are moral and social. Look at the causes and consequences of stress discussed earlier in this chapter. It is the elimination of stress rather than the medical cure of stress that will really improve the health of the nation.

Finally, Kennedy (1981: 166) says we must unmask medicine to dispel myths. There must be a new relationship between doctors and patients. We must take responsibility for our lives. Doctors must be made accountable (see also Illich 1977).

6 The Manufacture of Mental Illness

Szasz (1971) suggests that, whereas in the past people created witches, now they create mental patients. These would include people who transgress the morals of society – drug addicts, for example, or mothers who neglect their newborn babies. When people are classified as addicts or as mentally ill, they may be subject to involuntary hospitalization and treatment.

These people do not choose the role of mental patient. They are defined and treated as mental patients against their will. In short, the role is ascribed to them. On the other hand some people actually seek the role of mental patient – for example, a man trying to avoid military service. They assume the role of mental patient as the price they must pay for the service of an expert who can define the person as having a mental illness.

Laing (1971b: 3) has studied the effects of schizophrenia on the family. About 1 per cent of the population are affected by it, yet psychiatrists have struggled for years to discover what those who are so diagnosed have in common. There is no agreed way of diagnosing schizophrenia, no consistent theory, no agreement that it is a disease; no organic changes have been noted following post-mortems. Are we again 'constructing' a disease here?

Laing argues that the patient is not suffering from a disease whose outline is unknown. He or she is someone who acts in an odd way and becomes 'schizophrenic' after diagnosis and treatment. Even so a diagnosis is only a hypothesis, not a fact. Laing concludes that the behaviour of schizophrenia is much more intelligible than psychiatrists have supposed.

Is schizophrenia a disease or a social condition?

7 Conclusions

The following comparison between the viewpoints of the layperson and of the sociologist on illness and health should help the reader to identify the main conclusions of this chapter.

The layperson's view	*A sociological view*
We do not know when we are going to die. We do not know when disease is going to strike.	But we can improve our prospects of a long life. The enemy of this is poverty, which prevents many living the good life.
Class is less important now; we are all middle class now. Sociologists exaggerate the importance of class.	Class is still with us. Poorer people definitely have a shorter life expectancy (see preceding chapter). The gap between rich and poor has widened.

What does it matter if class persists? We all lead longer, healthier lives now.

As mentioned, the poor have a lower life expectancy – also a higher mortality ratio on all major diseases including heart disease (the so-called rich man's disease) and also a higher infant mortality ratio.

'Stress' is one of the 'in' words now – it is really indefinable. We must learn to put up with a bit of stress in life.

Stress kills. Stress is avoidable. Stress can be measured roughly (see Mitchell's eight dimensions of stress), and the poor suffer greater stress.

For better health we need more doctors and hospitals, etc.

We do need more medical resources but we should also invest more in preventative medicine – health education, meals on wheels, etc. Better still, we should aim for greater equality and less poverty. This would improve the nation's health more than wonder cures.

There's no such thing as society, only individuals and families (Margaret Thatcher cited in *New Statesman and Society*, 2 October 1992, p. 12).

Durkheim's study of suicide shows the importance of society in influencing the individual. Those more closely attached to the group (or society) were less liable to commit suicide.

Accidents will happen!

Accidents are often the results of our greed – step up production; cut down costs including safety measures.

The behaviour of drug addicts is 'senseless'. Why should they injure their health for temporary pleasure?

No behaviour is 'senseless' to the sociologist. Where the layperson gives up (explaining) the sociologist starts. In Becker's view the 'insiders' form their own group (or deviant subculture) and the mainstream are viewed as the outsiders. (The same applies to hard drinkers and heavy smokers and perhaps people who don't take precautions against AIDS.)

Illness is a physical thing. It can be measured (as in epidemiology, post-mortems and individuals' health and life expectancy).	Illness can be socially manufactured, as shown in this chapter.

Questions

Self-examination questions

(The answers may be found in the text.)

What is meant by the following?

- stress
- type-A man or woman
- life events
- the rules of sociological method
- deviant subculture

- the Black Report
- *The Health Divide*
- *Inequalities of Health*
- role conflict
- the social construction of illness

Essay or discussion questions

1 Who gets ill?
 Suggestion See Mitchell (1984: 2–7) for a discussion of groups at risk.

2 What do the Black Report and *the Health Divide* tell us about contemporary British society?
 Suggestions The reports highlight inequalities in Britain, including

inequalities of income, living conditions, and so on. These inequalities lead on to inequalities in health – the poor often get the least help (see previous chapter).

3   Why do people take risks with their health, especially drug taking?
Suggestions   See Becker (1963) on deviant subcultures. The sub-group, e.g. drug takers, regard the main group in society as being the outsiders.

4   What would you say are the central themes of this chapter?
Suggestions   (a) Inequalities in society and inequalities of health. (b) The hidden causes of ill-health, disability and early death. These themes are continuations from the previous chapter.

---

5   Read the extract and answer the questions that follow.

'Stress blamed for teachers' health problems'

Sickness and absenteeism among teachers, caused by stress, is costing millions of pounds a year, the Health and Safety Commission warned yesterday.

In a booklet on how to manage stress – which it says is the main health problem affecting teachers – the commission lists causes such as changes in working practices, long hours, a low perceived status, teaching mixed ability groups and threats of violence.

Peter Ward, West Midlands area director of the Health and Safety Executive and chairman of the commission group which compiled the report, said: 'The first important step is for education sector management to recognise that stress is not an indication of weakness or incompetence.

'Though it is difficult to estimate the prevalence of stress in the education sector alone, it is estimated that in all organisations up to 10 per cent of employees may suffer serious occupational stress, and up to 30 per cent may be affected in some way. It is essential for management to acknowledge that pressure of work can . . . trigger illness, and then . . . draw up action plans with staff.'

Stuart Nattrass, chairman of the advisory committee, told a confer-ence in Birmingham that managers who adopted a 'pull your socks up' approach were likely to aggravate the problem.

Instead, they should encourage staff to discuss problems and develop a 'caring culture' in schools. 'Do not leave individuals to cope alone or sweep it under the carpet as a sign of failure,' Mr Nattrass said.

Elaine Darbyshire, principal officer of the National Union of Teachers, who was a member of the working group, said more than 200 teachers leave the profession each term because of stress. 'Research has shown that one in three teachers were at burn-out level,' she said. 'This booklet will help people come out with the problem in the staff room.'

Managing occupational stress: A guide for managers and teachers in the schools sector. Educational Service Advisory Committee, HMSO.
(from Paul Hoyland, *Guardian*, 17 November 1990)

(a)   What are the causes and consequences of stress in schools?
(b)   What can doctors do about it?
(c)   What can sociologists do about it?

Suggestion   Sociologists can show that stress arises from lack of colleague support at work and too much control by management (see also chapter 3). There is a paradox here. Many teachers may cherish the freedom and independence of the job, yet feel it difficult to consult colleagues for fear of losing that independence.

---

6   What does the table 6.4 (opposite) tell us about the health of employees in different grades of the Civil Service?

---

7   To the sociologist accidents are not always a matter of random behaviour, a case of hard luck for the victim. Rather, accidents are caused, and it is the task of the sociologist to seek the cause – not just the obvious cause but the underlying social cause of the accident. The next example perhaps illustrates this. Read the extract and answer the questions that follow.

Jammed machine gave woman 4000 volt shock

A woman was electrocuted after receiving a shock of at least 4000 volts when she tried to free a jammed factory machine just 24 hours

Table 6.4 Percentage of men reporting selected psycho-social characteristics according to grade of employment in the British Civil Service

Characteristics	Administration	Professional/ executive	Clerical officers	Others
Type-A behaviour	61	46	30	27
Social support				
See confidant daily	92	86	82	80
No contact with relatives	15	17	20	22
No contact with neighbours	37	40	55	69
No social contact with people at work	55	66	72	82
No contact with other friends	20	22	20	40
Job attitudes				
Under-use of skills	50	58	68	67
Little or no control	7	14	18	33
Not fair treatment	11	16	16	33
No variety	0	4	21	37
Job of little value	2	2	6	9
Activities outside work				
Involved hobbies – solitary	46	36	26	20
Organized social-sedentary	45	39	30	29
Active, not vigorous exercise	85	86	62	40
Active sports	39	32	24	33

Source: Marmot (1987)

before ordered safety work was due to start, an inquest was told yesterday.

Therase Styles, a mother of four, had gone behind a protective screen to rectify what fellow workers claimed was a regular fault on the production line making magnetrons used in microwaves at the Sanyo factory at Thornaby, Cleveland.

Workers told the inquest at Teesside coroner's court, Middlesbrough, that instruction booklets for the machines were in Japanese, and the manager, Saboru Tanabe, could not speak fluent English even though he was responsible for warning staff about the high voltages.

Health and Safety Inspectors gave Sanyo three months to carry out safety measures after a visit in May 1989. The work was scheduled for July 19, the day after Mrs Styles, of Stockton, was killed. In June Sanyo was fined £4,000 after pleading guilty to two offences relating to the accident.

Elizabeth Hartley, an assembly worker, said the production line would break down on average 10 times a day when magnetrons became jammed in the robots which assembled the parts in a screened-off area. If the supervisor or Mr Tanabe was not around, workers would go behind the screen and move the magnetrons.

'Mr Tanabe was the only one who really understood the machine,' Mrs Hartley said. 'He was difficult to understand . . . I did not know how much voltage it was carrying, and no one told us not to go behind the screen.'

On the day of the accident she said, she could see there were two magnetrons in the test area. 'Therase went behind the screen and took one of the magnetrons out. I was going to take the other one out, as I was nearer. I said leave it, but she didn't answer me.'

Another worker, Karen Payne, said assembly girls regularly went behind the screens.

Mr Tanabe, aged 27, who spoke through an interpreter, told the coroner, Michael Sheffield, that workers were told not to go behind the screens, and he did not realise that they did. He said he told workers about the high voltage.

Mr Sheffield said: 'It's hard to believe Mrs Styles would have done what she did if she knew about the voltage.'

He added: 'Communication is important, and it would certainly seem that that was difficult in the case of Mr Tanabe, and maybe only limited instructions were given.'

The jury returned a verdict of accidental death caused by electrocution.

Afterwards Mrs Styles' husband, Joe, said he would take legal action against Sanyo.

A Sanyo spokesman said: 'It is tragic that this accident occurred shortly prior to the implementation of additional safety equipment recommended by the Health and Safety Executive.' (from *Guardian*, 22 September 1990)

(a) What are the apparent causes of this accident?
(b) What are the deeper causes (if any) of this accident?
(c) Why is this accident of interest to the sociologist?

Suggestions It seems that short cuts are being taken to keep production going at all costs; thus people are going behind the safety screens in order to rectify faults. The safety officer is also the production officer. There seems to be a role conflict here. The production officer tries to keep production going in order to achieve a high output, while a safety officer's first aim is safety.

8 Analyse the following extract from the viewpoint of the clinician, nurse, manager and sociologist.

Suggestions
- You may find useful the writings of Illich, Kennedy, Inglis and Freidson.
- We should take full account of the trauma involved in 'heroic' surgery (who is the 'hero'?)
- Are we being blinded by science?

Bypass surgery

During the 1970s, coronary care units gradually came to be over-shadowed by intensive care units, where, after the initial setback over heart transplants, the surgeons were enjoying an unexpected but very welcome bonanza.

Since early in the century a variety of surgical operations had been experimented with to treat angina, enthusiastic reports about their benefits being invariably followed by disillusionment and eventual discontinuance because of the high mortality rate. The first successful by-pass treatment, with the help of a vein grafted on the artery, was carried out in 1967; inevitably the achievement was overshadowed by Barnard's heart transplant the same year. Once mastered, however, the operation proved relatively simple, and the fact that veins could be taken from the patient's own body meant that there was no graft-rejection problem. Soon, reports came in of patients who had suffered agonies from angina getting up and about again, taking exercise and enjoying life. Surely, it was argued, as their coronary blood-flow was restored, the risk of a heart attack must also be reduced? The cardiac surgeons made the most of the opportunity. In 1971, 20,000 by-pass operations were performed in the United States; by 1973 the number had risen to 38,000.

To equip and run intensive and coronary care units was extremely expensive, the manufacturers of the required gadgetry seized their opportunity, competing energetically for sales. Cardiologists were easily persuaded that their units would be incomplete without the latest invention; that they could be criticised, and perhaps sued, for not using it; that they would be made to look foolish when they found that colleagues (and rivals) in nearby hospitals had had it installed; that it was their duty to their patients – and so on. As cardiologists wielded great influence, and as their units brought prestige to a hospital, the sale would often go through. But there was no way of telling how effective the gadget would be, other than the promise in the promotional hand-outs and the company representatives' sales-talk. 'With literally hundreds of companies competing for a share of the market for such devices as electro-cardiographs, defibrilators, and patient monitors', the Ehrenreich's report on behalf of the New York Health Policy Advisory Center warned in 1970, 'the average hospital administrator or the average physician is in no position to determine whether a particular feature of one model which adds several hundred dollars to the cost is really important, or whether it is merely the medical electronics equivalent of a chromium tail fin.'

Besides, the expense remained of little concern to American administrators, because 'in the final analysis the hospitals don't pay the bill, anyhow'. The cost had to be met by the patients, either directly or through insurance.

Were these units really in the best interests of patients? In 1971 Edith Heideman, Chief Nurse of the Henry Ford Hospital in Detroit, recalled how the first intensive-care unit had been set up twenty years before to provide special attention for patients recovering from serious operations, in particular open-heart surgery. In the course of the intervening two decades, she lamented, the concept had been utterly subverted. The center of attention was no longer the patient, but the gauges monitoring his blood pressure, heart-beat, fluid balance: 'banks of instruments that click, blink, or beep with (or without) the slightest provocation'. Patients who needed further attention, she found, were now afraid to return. 'I do not say that this is "unfortunate". I state flatly that it is criminal.'

In Britain, too, the new intensive-care units had begun to arouse concern. The aim of the medical profession, the London psychiatrist

Eliot Slater argued in an article 'Health Service or Sickness Service' in the *British Medical Journal* in 1971, should be to restore and maintain health, and, failing that, to relieve, or at least alleviate, suffering. The aim should not be the preservation of life at all costs, for if the first two aims were fulfilled, that could be left to look after itself. 'Per se, it is not part of a doctor's ordinary duties.' This was being forgotten; instead, Slater feared, there was likely to be a further expansion of units for intensive care, haemodialysis and organ transplants because they 'claim very high prestige, and are the pride of their mother hospitals'.

In 1972 another critic, R. S. Blacher of the Mount Sinai School of Medicine, New York, drew attention to a side-effect of open-heart surgery which the surgeons had not allowed for: out of twelve patients referred to him following operations, eight had 'suffered a major psychiatric upheaval, and yet had managed to hide this from their medical attendants'. To confess neurosis, in such circumstances, would have seemed base ingratitude; it was easier for patients to accept the assurance that they were doing fine – which, from the point of view of a surgeon primarily interested in their physical survival, they might be. C. D. Aring, a member of the editorial board of the *Journal of the American Medical Association*, admitted in the *Journal* in 1974 that a brief experience in an intensive-care unit had led him to believe that 'one should not want to be among its clientele unless profoundly unconscious' (from Inglis 1981).

---

9   Read the passage and answer the questions that follow.

In the High Street there are three furniture shops. Behind one window, a cardboard notice propped on the arm of a settee offers easy terms: buy now, pay later. During shopping hours, kitchen chairs and coffee tables spill out on to the street, secured by thin metal chains. Among these pavement bargains there are always two or three folding beds. Some have thin mattresses only an inch or two wide. The ones with thick mattresses have woodgrain formica shelves across the top.

People buy the fold-up beds because where they live there is not enough space for everyone to have their own proper bed. Each year the council housing waiting list gets longer. At the moment, to get a flat you need more than a hundred points. A woman, a man and two children living in two rooms may qualify after five years. Those in better conditions must wait a lifetime, living meanwhile with other members of the family or in private rented rooms. The landlords charge around £20 a week for two rooms, one with a sink and a stove in it, and the use of a shared bathroom and toilet.

After a year of campaigning, some of the terraced houses once owned by the private landlords have been bought up by the council. For the same rent you get more space and your own kitchen and bathroom. But often the conversions have been done on the cheap. The council is slow to carry out repairs on leaking roofs and fallen ceilings.

Beyond the terraced streets, over a mile from the shops, are the big estates. The biggest, a maze of interlocking giant blocks in barren yellow earth, was first planned in the early 1960s. The scheme looked so grim that the councillors threw it out. Four years later, in the face of growing waiting lists and dwindling resources, it was revived. Now it has become a place where only the most desperate live. Anxiety is a way of life. The old and chronically ill worry about being stranded when the lifts break down. There is always the fear that young children playing indoors will fall from the windows. They cannot play outside unless you go with them. In the anonymous open spaces, long corridors and empty car parks, there is no one to witness attacks on women, black people and the elderly.

Another estate of shining white concrete has just been completed. The flats have been designed with all-electric heating. The bills are much more than most tenants can afford. The tenants' association has won a rebate from the council, but still older people will not use the heating. In the winter they go to the library during the day, and in the evening they sit in their coats by single-bar electric fires. Many younger people are in debt. Those who have had the electricity disconnected cook by candle light on camping stoves loaned by social services. The children are cold. Sometimes there are fires (from Mitchell 1984: 13–14).

(a)   What are the health hazards in the situation described above?
(b)   How might a doctor or nurse analyse the situation?
(c)   How might a sociologist analyse this situation?

Further Reading

See Bibliography for full details.

J. Domanion, *Depression* (1976).

I. Kennedy, *The Unmasking of Medicine* (1981).

J. Mitchell, *What is to be Done about Illness and Health?* (1984).

M. Morgan, M. Calnan and N. Manning, *Sociological Approaches to Health and Medicine* (1985).

D. Patrick and G. Scambler (eds), *Sociology as Applied to Medicine* (1986).

P. Townsend and N. Davidson (eds), *Inequalities in Health* (1988).

M. Whitehead, *The Health Divide* (1988).

7 The National Health Service: A Sociological View

1 Introduction

This survey of the national health service is applicable within and beyond Britain. The questions it arouses could apply to other nations' health services. For instance: who shall manage the NHS? What group should it be? The general managers? The doctors and consultants? The nurses and senior nursing officers?

The next section asks how the NHS should be managed. Should there be two boards, one to set policy, the other to carry it out? Taking these questions more deeply, it could be asked what is the basic philosophy of the NHS and of the government's policy on the NHS? It is suggested that there are two main and opposing values or ideologies in the NHS. These are individualism (where individuals buy the services they require in the market) and universalism (where the patient is given the necessary treatment regardless of ability to pay). This is set out in table 7.1.

In the following section the future of the NHS is discussed. Probably this could be seen in terms of the continuing conflict between individualism and universalism, with the question of costs in the forefront of any discussion.

2 Who Should Manage the NHS?

Sir Roy Griffiths, after a review of the NHS in the 1980s, suggested that the government set up two boards. One should be a supervisory board to determine overall objectives and set the budget. This board would be established by the Secretary of State for Health. Then there would be an NHS management board accountable to the supervisory board whose chairperson was to come from general management and should be experienced in changing a large service-based organization to a managerial organization. In order to achieve credibility and establish a new management style, the new manager should come from outside the ranks of the Civil Service or NHS.

The team preparing the Griffiths Report (DHSS 1983) advocated closer involvement of doctors at local level but less time to be spent by doctors at meetings. The team thought there was a lack of incentive in the present system and an inability of chairpersons to reward merit or take action on ineffective performance. There was a need to increase productivity and reward skill. In the private sector all results would, it was thought, be carefully monitored against predetermined standards, since business people seem to have a keen sense of how well they are looking after their customers. The report also stressed that the NHS had to balance the interests of patient, community, taxpayer and employee, and that it should rigorously prune many of its existing services.

Although this report may have appeared to be neutral there were possibly some hidden assumptions about the nature of management. For example, why was it recommended that the new NHS managers should come from outside the Civil Service? Some of the most efficient managers are civil servants. The call for the closer involvement of doctors at local level in fact relegates doctors to local level (and out of management). Allowing managers to reward merit, etc., gives more power to management. The idea that the NHS must balance interests also gives managers much extra power. It leaves the decision-making in the hands of unelected managers.

The question of pruning services again causes problems. To take one example: to sub-contract catering in a hospital may make financial sense but it may be detrimental to the personal relationship between catering staff, nurses and patients.

The Griffiths Report seems to have assumed that the health service should be run by general managers rather than by doctors, consultants and nurses; and that the principles of general management can be applied to a non-commercial organization like the health service. Table 7.1 seeks to analyse some of these beliefs and assumptions.

Table 7.1   Individualism and universalism

Treatment based on value for money and on individualism	Treatment based on principles of welfare – especially 'universalism'
Treatment to be based on costs and/or on ability to pay.	Free treatment regardless of cost.
Aim – primarily value for money.	Aim – good health.
Leave it to the market to decide what to provide and at what price.	Leaving it to the market implies that the government need do nothing, but individuals have needs including the need for good health, and these needs must be met regardless of what the market says.
Beds may have to be cut to save money.	Cutting beds is a waste. The skilled staff are available but are not being used.
Use sub-contractors for non-medical work such as cleaning and catering in hospitals.	Sub-contractor's staff are not really part of the organization's staff and hence there may be some social distancing between nurses, non-medical staff and patients.
People should not run to the state for help.	Agreed! But people may need help.

3   The Future of the NHS

The National Health Service Act came into force in the UK in 1948 and was based on universalism (see Glossary), on the principle of health care at the point of need. Treatment was to be free regardless of cost. Since the 1940s, however, Britain seems to have lost much of the reforming zeal of wartime, especially where reforms have to be paid for in taxes. The costs are increasing because the population is getting older and because, as medicine advances, it becomes more expensive.

Although the NHS is still popular with patients and the public, governments have sought means of cutting health costs. One method is the system of the 'internal market' consisting of the providers of services, like the big hospitals, and the purchasers of services, like doctors, who identify needs. Other reforms that have been introduced include GPs having their own budgets and hospitals becoming self-governing NHS trusts.

A sociology of health services

So far it has been shown that the NHS is being extensively reformed and that an internal market for health services is being established. As mentioned, there seem to be two main values in the health service, individualism and universalism (Segalman and Marsland 1989). Now a sociological view of the administration will be taken in order to highlight still further hidden values, assumptions and ideologies, showing where the sociologist can give a clearer view of what is happening. Cox (1991) is very useful in providing some of these insights.

From administration to management

When the national health service was established it was assumed it would have clinical autonomy and expertise. It would be an organization in which administration rather than management would be the key concept. This was because the NHS was based on a large number of independent units which were run on a routine basis; management skills were not so necessary then. Against this background, Griffiths took the radical step of introducing general management into the NHS.

The centrality of management Although the NHS is vast, employing over one million people in 1989, it is surprising that its management has not until recently been a central issue, for example in relation to questions of resources, planning, capital development, etc. – and who actually decides planning. In so far as there are ideologies, it is the ideology of the small business that has been the centre of attention.

The implementation of the Griffiths Report   Under the terms of the Griffiths report, general management jobs are to be open to clinicians (but there was little demand for them). The reaction of the nursing profession, especially from nurse managers who were largely ignored by the Griffiths Report, was very critical. Indeed, the Royal College of Nursing conducted an advertising campaign seeking support from all those who understood nursing (Clay 1987).

The general managers   Griffiths (DHSS 1983) argued that the health service needed a change in its culture rather than a reorganization. General management roles were to be charted. In fact, it is not easy to create new ways of thinking, as the studies of the socialization of doctors and nurses in chapter 2 indicated.

Administration   The Institute of the Health Service Administration, on publication of the Griffiths Report, changed its name to the Institute of Health Service Management, thus emphasizing the transition from administration to management. In practice, health service managers sometimes found themselves competing against general managers. Mere administration was abolished. In its place came management (Strong and Robinson 1988: 56).

Nurses

Nurses account for half the labour force of the NHS (Cox 1991: 101). Nurses have tried to preserve routes into both general management and district health authorities. Griffiths concentrated on the new managers, but said little about nurses. On the other hand, it is nurses at ward level who are under management pressure for greater productivity (Cox 1991: 103).

Doctors

Cox suggests that the desire to obtain some management control of doctors was the principal objective of the Griffiths Report (Cox 1991: 103). Strong and Robinson (1988) claim that in the past the medical role had been secure; the doctors were powerful, and this weakened other groups in the health service. At present the new general managers' powers over consultants are still very limited. It seems that doctors and consultants have considerable influence in the health service, for example in acquiring new equipment. However, the effect of an 'internal market' with hospital trusts may be to weaken the powers of the doctors and consultants.

4 Satisfaction with the NHS

Owing mainly to underfunding, there has been a growing dissatisfaction with the NHS. As mentioned, the British government's response to the dissatisfaction was to set up internal markets in the NHS, to take on more general managers and to encourage private health care.

In spite of some dissatisfaction, however, the British public would like health to have a high priority. Surveys in 1983 and 1987 presented people with a list of items of government expenditure and asked them which, if any, would be their highest priority for extra spending. The responses are shown in table 7.2.

Table 7.2 Public views of government spending priorities

First priority	1983 (%)	1987 (%)
Health	37	52
Education	24	24
Help for industry	16	5
Housing	7	8
Social security benefits	6	4

Source: Jowell et al. (1988: 95)

Table 7.3   Support for the universal NHS, 1983–1987

	1983 (%)	1987 (%)
Social class		
I/II	70	72
III non-manual	67	70
III manual	60	68
IV/V	60	65
Household income		
Highest 25%	72	68
Middle 50%	64	72
Low 25%	57	66

Source: Jowell et al. (1988: 97)

Table 7.3 demonstrates the strength of support for the NHS. Indeed it is strongest among the wealthiest sections of the population. (It does not make much difference to the result whether social class or income is used to measure the respondent's wealth.) Tables 7.4 and 7.5 show the areas of dissatisfaction with the NHS.

Table 7.4   Satisfaction with branches of the NHS

	Satisfied ('very'/'quite') (%)	Neither/ don't know (%)	Dissatisfied ('very'/'quite') (%)
Local doctors/GPs	79	8	13
National health service dentists	74	17	9
Health visitors	46	45	8
District nurses	55	41	3
Being in hospital as an in-patient	67	19	13
Attending hospital as an out-patient	54	18	29

Source: Jowell et al. (1988: 100)

Table 7.5 Where improvement is needed

	In need of improvement ('a lot' or 'some') (%)
Hospital waiting lists for non-emergency operations	87
Waiting time before getting appointments with hospital consultants	83
Staffing levels of nurses in hospitals	75
Staffing levels of doctors in hospitals	70
Hospital casualty departments	54
General condition of hospital building	53
GPs' appointment systems	47
Amount of time GP gives to each patient	33
Quality of medical treatment in hospitals	30
Being able to choose which GP to see	29
Quality of medical treatment by GPs	26
Quality of nursing care in hospitals	21

Source: Jowell et al. (1988: 101)

5 Conclusions

With the establishment of 'internal markets' and greater autonomy of local management, sociologists should study the management of health care. There is a need for more case studies.

What are the effects of the new-style management – perhaps not all that obvious so far?

We should always be on guard where values and beliefs are being used to justify actions, for example, the scientific ideologies of the managers (see Glossary for a discussion of *scientific management*).

Other key issues include the conflict between universalism and individualism; the contrast between administration and management; the future of the NHS and the internal market and the status of nursing organization.

An important theme of this chapter is the practice of management in the NHS. Most of the questions that follow give an opportunity to the reader to demonstrate administrative or management or nursing skills. However, the emphasis must be on objective research, not on journalistic exposés.

Questions

Self-examination questions

What are the following?

- a supervisory board
- a management board
- internal market
- provider of services
- purchaser of services
- GP's budget
- NHS trust

- scientific management
- universalism
- individualism
- management and administration
- professional ideology
- cure ideology

Essay or discussion questions

1   Referring to the article that follows, what do you think is the basic problem here and what can be done about it?

NHS bed closures 'meant delay for 340,000 operations'

By Health Services Correspondent Jack O'Sullivan

More than 9,000 National Health Service hospital beds were closed at some stage last year, a survey by the British Medical Association has found.

Of these nearly 3,250 beds were permanently closed because of cash shortages and 4,400 were closed temporarily. The remaining 1,520 were part of rationalisation programmes.

If the 3,250 beds had remained open, 340,000 extra operations could have been performed, cutting waiting lists by a third, the BMA estimates.

Last night, Robin Cook, Labour's health spokesman, described the closures 'a staggering rate of loss', worse than the 1987 crisis, which prompted the Government to inject £100m into the health service.

Stephen Dorrell, a health minister, said that the closures were in line with a long-term decline in the number of NHS acute beds, going back to 1974. He said that the fall reflected improvements in modern medicine meaning that recovery was quicker.

The report also found between 10 and 15 per cent of patients had to wait for more than two years for treatment in South-West Thames, South-East Thames and North-West Thames. Between 5 and 10 per cent of patients had to wait for more than two years for treatment in Yorkshire, Northern, Trent, Wessex, East Anglian, South Western, West Midlands, North Western and Oxford.

Use of NHS operating theatres in England: a progress report, HMSO £5.50. (from *Independent*, 22 March 1991)

Suggestions It seems beds are lying empty because operations are not being performed. In some parts of the country, waiting lists are very much higher than in others. This problem could be tackled by spending more money on the NHS.

Basically it depends on what your values are. Do you believe that health care should be provided to all according to need and regardless of ability to pay (universalism)? Or do you believe that too much welfare (welfareism) weakens the will of individuals to make their own way in the world? Thus universalism and welfareism could be looked upon as ideologies justifying levels of action.

See also Segalman and Marsland (1989) for the individualistic view of welfare.

---

2   Analyse table 7.6. What trends can be deduced from it?

Suggestions The table seems to show little increase in staff numbers in the health service. In fact the total of national health service staff fell by 3 per cent between 1981 and 1989. There were increases in some qualified staff; for example, numbers of medical and dental staff increased by 11 per cent. On the other hand, ancillary staff numbers fell by 38 per cent because of the privatizing of laundry, catering and

Table 7.6 Manpower in the health and personal social services,[a] United Kingdom (thousands)

Regional and district health authorities	1981	1984	1985	1986	1987	1988	1989
Medical and dental (excluding locums)	49.7	51.4	52.1	52.4	52.0	53.7	55.0
Nursing and midwifery (excluding agency staff)	492.8	500.8	505.1	505.6	507.3	507.6	509.0
Professional and technical	80.2	89.2	91.2	93.4	96.8	98.0	99.7
Administrative and clerical	133.3	135.5	136.7	137.2	141.2	142.9	149.4
Ancillary	220.1	198.1	184.1	167.4	156.6	146.4	136.1
Other non-medical	56.2	55.4	55.1	55.0	54.4	52.4	50.8
Total health service staff	1032.2	1030.4	1024.3	1011.0	1008.3	1001.0	1000.0
Family practitioner services	53.3	58.2	59.3	57.3	58.4	59.3	59.8
Personal social services							
Social work staff	28.4	30.1	30.8	32.2	33.4	34.6	
Managerial, administration and ancillary	27.7	29.1	29.5	30.4	32.0	32.9	
Other[b]	194.8	207.1	211.8	217.7	222.7	226.3	
Total personal social services staff	250.9	266.3	272.2	280.3	288.2	293.9	

[a]Figures for family practitioner services are numbers; all other figures are whole-time equivalents.
[b]Includes home help service and other community support staff, day care, residential day care and other staff.

Source: Social Trends (1991). Department of Health; Welsh Office; Scottish Health Service, Common Services Agency; Scottish Education Department, Social Works Services Group; Department of Health and Social Services, Northern Ireland.

domestic services. It does not seem that expenditure on the NHS has got out of hand.

---

3   What is wrong in the situation described below, and what would you do about it?

Old people in homes face increasing fees burden

By David Fletcher, Social Services Correspondent

Families responsible for elderly relatives in residential homes face intolerable pressure meeting the weekly difference between fees charged and social security benefits, says a report published yesterday.

Counsel and Care, a charity providing help and advice for the elderly, says the gap was as much as £70 a week for some older people. Old people were often unable to find the money, their families could not afford it and they were forced to turn to charities.

Counsel and Care devotes nearly £100,000 a year to ease the situation, but this year's budget is already spent. A spokesman said 'We are operating a waiting list. We are not alone, as other funds report they simply cannot meet the demands placed upon them because of the inadequate levels of benefit.'

The charity says a good room in a private nursing home in London costs up to £360 a week. A private residential care home costs up to £245.

Although cheaper accommodation could be found in London, the minimum was £305 a week in a private nursing home and £213 in a private residential care home – well above Income Support levels.

From next week, when payments rise, the maximum help is £288 for anyone in a nursing home in London and £183 for an elderly person in a residential home (from *Daily Telegraph*, 4 April 1991).

Suggestions
- In the long run all property prices will rise including those of nursing homes residential care homes.
- One of the main problems is the inadequate level of benefits to pay the charges.

- It is important that the price of care in the community should not be too high, in view of the increasing number of patients being discharged, many with chronic diseases and disabilities.

---

4   Who orders expensive equipment in the hospital? Is it the doctor or the manager? Why do not all those who can benefit actually benefit? Try to quote examples to illustrate the following newspaper report.

Breathing aid plea to save lung patients

By our Health Service Correspondent

Tens of thousands of people with chronic lung disorders risk dying prematurely because they are not given oxygen therapy, lung specialists said yesterday.

Launching a 'Breathe Easy' club for sufferers, the British Lung Foundation said about one million people in Britain lived with bronchitis, emphysema and other disabling breathing problems, yet oxygen therapy was prescribed to only 5,000.

Dr John Moore-Gillon, consultant lung specialist, said the treatment would improve the quality of life and life expectancy of about 50,000–60,000 patients.

'Many of them are reluctant to seek help from their doctor because they feel there is a stigma attached to lung disease and that to admit to it is a step downhill,' he said.

'We want to overcome that stigma and encourage doctors to refer more people with obstructive airways diseases to lung specialists who can assess whether oxygen therapy will help them.'

Mr Trevor Clay, president of the club and former general secretary of the Royal College of Nursing who retired early because of emphysema, called for more oxygen therapy to be available on the NHS.

He said portable systems were needed so that people could lead a normal life rather than become house bound (from *Daily Telegraph*, 3 April 1981).

Suggestions   Probably it is the doctor or consultant who asks for the latest equipment. This is backed up by the doctor's clinical judgement which the manager is not in a position to challenge. Note the effect of stigma mentioned in the extract – this is also dealt with in Goffman (1983).

---

5   After reading the extract answer these questions.

(a) Is it possible to abolish the giant private health insurance industry in Britain and in the United States?
(b) Why should one want to do this?
(c) What would you replace it with?
(d) How can the poor be protected by private health insurance?

Private health insurance

Perhaps one of the arguments against a giant private health insurance company is that they become arbiters of welfare and that their interests are based on cash.

The argument that the insurance industry is too powerful is a strong weapon favoring the industry. A number of health policy analysts might privately state the United States needs a national health program in which private insurance is no longer part of the landscape. But publicly, such analysts support minor and unworkable reforms because they are afraid to advocate 'radical' positions. Yet if every influential person who privately favors a public single-payer health system would publicly state his or her support for such change, the idea would no longer be radical, but would enter the mainstream health policy debate.

Suppose a professor of medical care administration entered the classroom and described a country with the following characteristics. If you are healthy and have a high-paying job, you get health insurance; if you get so sick that you lose your job, you lose your insurance. If you have a low-paying job, and thus can least afford to pay for medical care, you get no health insurance. Private health insurers keep billions of dollars in administrative expenses and pro- fits. With all their money they hire lobbyists and make political cam- paign contributions in order to keep the system from changing. And in order to spare private health insurers the unprofitable problems of the elderly and the poor, taxpayers and wage-earners – in addition to paying for part of their own health coverage – pay for the care of these unprofitable groups. To which country does the professor refer? The United States of America (from Bodenheimer 1990).

---

6   What in your personal view has changed over the past ten years in the NHS and what has remained the same?

Continuity and change

It is worth reviewing for a moment how much has not changed. The NHS, as a national service with comprehensive aims and responsibilities, is still essentially intact. For example, reviewing the NHS in 1988, after the first wave of Conservative reforms, Robert Maxwell, Secretary of the King Edward's Hospital Fund for London, concluded:

- its institutional structure, with divisions between general practice, acute and chronic care, and between local health services and local authority services is essentially unchanged;
- after the first year or two of Mrs Thatcher's first administration, ideas for public insurance funding, as an alternative to general taxation, were quietly shelved; even the proposals to introduce a charge for the use of capital (to make people more aware that capital is not a 'free good') appear to have been laid aside;
- in the heartland of medical care, all major medical services are still free at the point of use;
- the professions – except for nursing at the senior level – have largely remained unchanged: many doctors seem barely to have heard of general management yet, let alone felt much effect from it;
- consumers have virtually the same (lack of) powers as before: for example it is not easier to change GPs;
- waiting times remain a severe problem for people needing cold surgery;
- such major policies for change as resource redistribution and the upgrading of priority services continue largely unaffected;
- although the private sector has grown quickly, in medical care it remains a small part of the total, with only 8 per cent of the population insured privately: the Government have actually done little to promote it, and where they have done so (in boarding-

out allowances for private residential care) the change seems to have arisen almost by accident.

In short the NHS, as it nears the forty mark and enters middle age is recognisably the same on the ground, for better, for worse, for richer, for poorer, as it was ten years earlier (from Maxwell 1988).

---

7   As a senior nurse, what improvement would you suggest for the administration or management of the NHS? Do nurses have ambitions to become part of management?

Suggestions
- You could use your hospital or organization as a specific example of the place.
- Are nurses socialized to their role as nurse (see chapter 2)?
- Describe organizations where there is less management and more emphasis on nursing skills, for example the hospice; hospitals which stress the nursing process, etc.

---

8   Answer the questions at end of the extract, using your own experience when possible.

Nurses face uncertainty

No organisational blueprint was proposed in the Griffiths Report. The main emphasis was on making the doctors both clinically and financially responsible and developing clear lines of accountability to the ultimate authority of the general manager. It was uncertain how this would work out in practice for the nurses, but this issue of professional accountability to a manager who was not a nurse was the first question to be raised.

The other principal theme, that of making the Service more efficient and cost-effective, also had ramifications for nurses. It was suggested that the management structure was top heavy, and that nurse manpower levels needed reassessment. This created major anxieties among the nurses in management who feared losing their jobs, and having their qualified staff replaced by cheaper, unskilled workers.

On both counts, the report was viewed as a threat – a dilution of the power, importance and value of nurses in the NHS.

Organisational change had preceded Griffiths' letter, but it was a transformation that continued at an accelerated pace after 1984, when his recommendations were implemented. The psychological effects of such drastic change on those working in the NHS cannot be overestimated. Reorganisation for many managers had meant seeing their colleagues phased out, or having to compete for their own jobs, or for fewer jobs. To some extent it explained a certain reluctance to undergo further change. . . .

Although Griffiths had not recommended further reorganisation, this did not quite equate to some of the other suggestions he was making. Reducing levels of staff in management, the introduction of general management above the levels necessary for functional management, and stringent cost-effectiveness drives made it seem inevitable that some restructuring would occur.

Even in situations where general managers preferred to leave their staff in relative peace, the future remained uncertain. What Griffiths had done was to open the door to endless possibilities, to raise the issue of change as a permanent feature of the Health Service's continuous need to adapt to external pressures in the face of rapid social and technological change.

At the same time, nursing had reached a crossroads. It was experiencing growing staffing difficulties. It was faced with a crisis of professional identity when the educational needs of nurses had not kept pace with sociological and technological change. Most of all, it was faced with a crisis of meaning in terms of nurses' place and value in modern society, and within our health care system today (from Owen and Glennerster 1990).

(a) How can doctors, managers and nurses be made more accountable for their work?
(b) Are the nurses' fears well founded?

Suggestions It might be useful to refer to professional and managerial ideologies. Use health service statistics and *Social Trends*.

9 Read the extract and tackle the arguments raised.

Political cripples

Medical charities are overly dazzled by the search for miracle cures to eliminate disability, says Andrew Tyler.

As that savage critic of industrial society, Ivan Illich, once remarked: 'Medical spectator sports cast powerful spells upon the public.' Illich described heart swap pioneer Dr Christiaan Barnard's visit to Brazil some years ago. In both Lima and Rio de Janeiro, he saw Barnard fill the major football stadiums twice in a single day with crowds who hysterically acclaimed the surgeon's ability to replace defective human hearts. They cheered even though most of them had no access to a neighbourhood clinic, much less to the kind of hospital in which organ transplantation could take place. They cheered, Illich writes in his classic Penguin paperback, *Medical Nemesis*, because Barnard provided them 'with an abstract assurance that salvation through science is possible'.

Here in the UK, we also look for salvation through science. We turn to our bio-medical priesthood for the defeat of natural processes, including the forestalling of death. And for most people, it is more thrilling to invest in bio-miracles than in commonplace strategies of healthy living and eating, even though an objective analysis of the record shows that industrial medicine's war against what have been called the 'disease of affluence' – cancer, heart disease, emphysema, diabetes, bronchitis – has been lost.

Yet the public exalts the technodocs as never before. Charities specialising in medical research have become financial giants. Research spending for 1990–91 was nearly £216 million – a jump on the previous year of £41 million; it has tripled in the past decade. The Imperial Cancer Research Fund is now the fourth-biggest earning charity in the country.

People pay not only because they seek quick-fix solutions to problems of infirmity and death, but also because the charities are increasingly adept at marketing guilt and fear. You are challenged to walk past a poster showing a shattered individual in a wheelchair, the suggestion being that unless you put money in the tin next time you see it, you wish that individual eternal misery. Then there is the Cancer Research Campaign's famous 'crossed-fingers' poster with the headline, '. . . or make a donation'. In other words: pay up or die.

And so the public pays. And money that should more logically go to the sufferers themselves – to make them more mobile; to compensate for earnings lost through disability – is going towards propping up the charities' own administrative bureaucracies, and into funding scientific research projects that frequently lead down irrelevant and/ or dangerous cul de sacs.

Arguments as to how money should be apportioned have sprung up within charities themselves, especially those with the double brief of supporting sufferers and research. One of the most public rows engulfed the Parkinson's Disease Society in December 1990, culminating in accusations of ballot-rigging and the sacking of its director. But while grassroots fundraisers often prefer more cash to be spent on welfare, the public apparently does not.

'It is research that brings the money in, not welfare,' says Diana Garnham, general secretary of the Association of Medical Research Charities (AMRC), a body representing 65 member organisations and affiliates. 'Research gets news coverage. Even the *Sun* covers research constantly. They're always talking in terms of breakthroughs, which is naive, but it's there. People absorb it and they want to give money. They won't give if you say we want to spend it on wheelchairs for people with Parkinson's disease.'

A growing number of those in whose name the research money is being raised – people with chronic disabling ailments – are beginning to baulk at this. Jane Campbell is joint chair of the British Council of Organisations of Disabled People, an umbrella group representing 120,000 people in 82 organisations.

'Disablement is a fact of life,' says Campbell. 'It will always exist. Yes, people will always look for some sort of cure, but the prospective cure for the neuro-muscular impairment I have is so far away and so entwined with the "perfect body" syndrome that I don't want anything to do with it. I prefer that society revised its infrastructure to accommodate people's differences, because you will always have people with disabilities, whether through illness, ageing, war or accident. To pretend disablement doesn't exist, or to try to get rid of it, is as bad as wanting to get rid of people who have different religious views or different behaviour patterns.' Research should 'relate to quality of life improvements such as pain relief and the kind of revolution in mobility that the provision of an electric wheelchair can bring' (from *New Statesman and Society*, 12 June 1992).

(a)   What is the gist of the argument?
(b)   Can there be salvation through science?
(c)   Account for the growth of the health climate.
(d)   Discuss the view that the disabled are always with us.
(e)   Should some work done by charities really be done by governments?
(f)   Any further questions?

Suggestions   Consult the normal accounts of leading health charities (use libraries). Which charities fare the best and why? It seems that money goes to popular charities, for example those researching cures for cancer, rather than more mundane concerns such as wheelchairs for the sufferers of Parkinson's disease. We do not know what the charities themselves want most of all, and this makes it harder for charities to forecast their plans.

---

10   Read the passage and answer the questions that follow.

Health status and quality of life

For many health problems treated by health services, not only is death an uncommon and inappropriate measure of outcome but also, more importantly, the primary purpose of treatment is to improve patient's functioning and well-being. Consider, for example, drug treatment for rheumatoid arthritis, epilepsy or migraine, hospice care of the terminally ill, or surgery for ulcerative colitis. In all such instances we are concerned with the broad, pervasive effects that health problems have on the patient in terms of pain, disability, anxiety, depression, social isolation, embarrassment, or difficulties in carrying on daily life. From the patient's perspective, health care is largely judged in terms of impact on these broader aspects of personal well-being. In recent years outcome measures have emerged in an attempt to capture such aspects of patients' experiences. Frequently termed quality-of-life measures, they may often also be referred to as health-status instruments.

The Karnofsky Performance Index

Description	Scale (%)
Normal, no complaints	100
Able to carry on normal activities; minor signs of symptoms of disease.	90
Normal activity with effort.	80
Cares for self. Unable to carry on normal activity or to do active work.	70
Requires occasional assistance but able to care for most of his needs.	60
Requires considerable assistance and frequent medical care.	50
Disabled; requires special care and assistance.	40
Severely disabled; hospitalization indicated although death not imminent.	30
Very sick. Hospitalization necessary. Active supportive treatment necessary.	20
Moribund.	10
Dead.	0

Source: Fallowfield (1990); Scambler (1991)

(a) What is meant by the quality of life?
(b) Can the quality of life be measured?

Suggestions
- Patients are living longer now.
- Different medicines are being used now.
- We must ensure that patients' last days are as comfortable as possible.
- Would you wish to alter the table?

Further Reading

See Bibliography for full details.

T. Bodenheimer, 'Should We Abolish the Private Health Insurance Industry?' (1990).

T. Clay, *Nurses: Power and Politics* (1987).

D. Cox, 'Health Service Management – A Sociological View' (1991).

DHSS, *NHS Management Enquiry: The Griffiths Report* (1983).

J. Gabe, M. Calnan and M. Bury (eds), *The Sociology of the Health Service* (1991).

R. Jowell, S. Witherspoon and L. Brook (eds), *British Social Attitudes – the 5th Report* (1988).

R. Maxwell (ed.), *Reshaping the National Health Service* (1988).

R. Segalman and D. Marsland, *From Cradle to Grave* (1989).

R. Titmuss, *Commitment to Welfare* (1968).

A. Tyler, 'Political Cripples' (1992).

8 Women, Health and Nursing

1 Introduction

Since women are still in the majority in the nursing profession, this chapter seeks to explore the inequalities that women experience in the family, in society and at work. Looking at the place of women in society generally, it can be seen that there is still a lot of prejudice against women. Over the period 1984–91 the gap between the earnings of men and women in the UK remained as great as ever. There still seems to be a strong feeling about what is women's work and what is not, despite the fact that women can do any sort of work. This chapter will also discuss women's different health requirements and family responsibilities.

Finally the future of the nursing profession is considered. Project 2000 envisages an all-graduate nursing profession in which students are supernumerary to NHS staffing throughout the whole period of probation. In other words, student nurses would no longer do the non-medical chores but would concentrate on their course work.

2 Women and Society

Many of the prejudices against women at work still abound, despite the setting up of the Equal Opportunities Commission in 1975. Table 8.1 shows there has been little progress in the fight for equal earnings.

Table 8.1 Weekly earnings of men and women: all occupations (pounds)

	1984	1991	Differences
Males	179	319	140
Females	117	174	57

Source: New Earnings Survey, Department of Employment (1984 and 1991)

Table 8.2 analyses the division of labour between men and women in the home. It shows that the majority of women still undertake most of the domestic work, and that this situation has not changed much in the period 1983–7.

3 'Women's Work'

In chapter 2 it was shown how students are socialized to the role of nurse. In addition, however, girls are also socialized to the role of woman, and indeed all the female roles, such as mother, wife, etc., which society expects women to perform. Salvage (1985) argues that most nurses are women and it is still regarded as a woman's job. Even today, says Salvage, female student nurses are told that their training is a good preparation for being a wife and mother. (Some women nurses might dispute this. What is your experience?) On the other hand she believes that better education for women generally has made nursing less appealing, and that many potential nurses are put off by its old-fashioned and stuffy image. Salvage then goes on to make the distinction between caring and curing (a theme of this book).

Men are often seen as 'rational' and decisive. Men are also seen as assertive and this is acceptable in men, whereas assertive women are regarded as aggressive. Again, doctors are seen as curers and scientists, while passive nurses give loving care. Salvage concludes that in reality work in health care does not divide in that way, but we have what amounts to a conspiracy of scientists to advance the myth.

The following two extracts from Salvage's book give some idea of frustrations in the nursing profession and their possible causes. They seem to illustrate how socialization courses can preserve the myth, thus leading to further frustration.

Table 8.2 The domestic division of labour

	1983 (%)	1987 (%)
Who:		
does household shopping?		
mainly man	5	7
mainly woman	51	50
shared equally	44	43
makes evening meal?		
mainly man	5	6
mainly woman	77	77
shared equally	17	17
does evening dishes?		
mainly man	17	22
mainly woman	40	39
shared equally	40	36
does household cleaning?		
mainly man	3	4
mainly woman	72	72
shared equally	24	23
does washing and ironing?		
mainly man	1	2
mainly woman	89	88
shared equally	10	9
repairs household equipment?		
mainly man	82	82
mainly woman	6	6
shared equally	10	8
organizes household money/bills?		
mainly man	29	32
mainly woman	39	38
shared equally	32	30
looks after sick children?		
mainly man		2
mainly woman		67
shared equally		30
teaches children discipline?		
mainly man		13
mainly woman		19
shared equally		67

Source: Jowell et al. (1988)

Frustration and helplessness

'Our training actively discourages us from discussing our work critically and encourages us to view our problems as individual failings. The classic incident occurred two wards back when sister took me into her office the day before I was due to leave, to ask me how I felt about the ward. She had decided I must be very unhappy as I did not appear to smile much, when in fact I had been perfectly content, though extremely harassed most of the time "trying to get the work done". So she asked my thoughts – and I told her. Sister listened attentively, though her face grew more and more stern, so I knew she was not taking kindly to what I said. She sharply asked how I could improve the situation, so I tentatively suggested that a bit more organization was needed. My reply from her was to the effect that I only had ten months' nursing experience, compared with her ten years, so anything I said was worthless and not worth discussing further. The following day I collected my report and discovered that I am a quiet, dour girl with little enthusiasm or motivation who is too critical of the running of the ward. It was at this stage that I could easily have packed it in because of my feelings of frustration and helplessness' (Salvage 1985: 56).

The 'ideal' recruit

A famous hospital specialist in London, when requesting references for potential new nursing staff, sends out a pre-printed letter to referees stating that 'good health is essential, a good education, also intelligence and common sense'.

It goes on: 'It is desirous that members of nursing staff should be of a patient, cheerful and kindly disposition, willing and able to apply themselves to their studies, and amenable to a reasonable degree of discipline.'

The letter then asks for assessments of the applicant under

these headings: general temperament and disposition, intelligence and capabilities, moral character (Salvage 1985: 56).

4 Women and Health

What special health requirements do women have that are different
from those of men? Are these being met? Is childbirth too technical
now? What can be done to improve communications between doctors
and women patients? These are some of the questions tackled in this
section.

Childbirth

Oakley (1980) shows that many mothers in her study felt depressed
after childbirth. There may be a number of reasons for this. First,
there may be too much emphasis on the technical aspects of childbirth
at the expense of the mother's feelings. Secondly, our culture tends
to emphasize conformity, maintaining the status quo and '*coping*' (stiff
upper lip, etc.). Thirdly, we tend to measure by purely medical
standards, for example infant mortality rather than the mother's
feelings. We therefore tend not to see the social factors of childbirth.
Oakley tries to objectify the social factors that may lead to depression
at childbirth. These are:

● being unemployed;
● having segregated marital roles (for example, the husband does
no housework);
● having a housing problem;
● having had no previous contact with babies.

Oakley calls these items 'vulnerability factors' and derives the data
presented in table 8.3. Oakley reports that 80 per cent of the mothers
said the whole process of childbirth was misrepresented and shown
as too romantic. The lack of realistic expectations made it all worse;

Table 8.3 Depression or depressed mood in relation to vulnerability factors at childbirth

No. of vulnerability factors	Depressed		Not depressed		Total	
	%	(N)	%	(N)	%	(N)
Four factors	100	(4)	0	(0)	100	(4)
Three factors	70	(7)	30	(3)	100	(10)
Two factors	53	(11)	47	(10)	100	(21)
One factor	20	(4)	80	(16)	100	(20)

Source: Oakley (1980: 172)

many women feel misled. Having a baby hurts more than they expected. Often they did not realize the extent of medical intervention, for example induced births, forceps delivery, and so on.

The role of motherhood is given by the culture, that is to say it is defined by men. Mothers are seen as all-sacrificing, and this becomes a learnt attitude. Similarly, mothers see girl infants as an extension of self, whereas boys are regarded as different and therefore made to feel different.

The following are some of Oakley's proposals for the redomestication of childbirth and perhaps a less depressed life for those women who encounter problems.

Birth

1 An end to unnecessary medical intervention in childbirth.

2 The redomestication of birth.

3 A return to female-controlled childbirth.

4 The provision of therapeutic support for women after childbirth.

Bringing up children

5 More state or community help for parents, and more state/community participation in childcare.

6 The abolition of fixed gender roles, especially in the family and pertaining to social parenthood.

7 Less segregation of children into homes, nurseries, schools, etc., and more integration of children with mainstream social concerns and activities.

8 Less privatization and isolation of families.

The wider context

9 The formal and informal teaching of realistic parenthood and childbirth to both females and males from infancy onwards.

10 Woman-centred and woman-controlled reproductive care.

11 Less cultural retreat from confrontation with pain and suffering.

12 The reduction of poverty and class-based inequalities.

The Well Woman Clinic

Gardner (1981: 130–3) argues the case for the Well Woman Clinic. She says that for several reasons women consult doctors more frequently than men do; for example, women assume the main responsibility for contraception, sick children and pregnancy advice. Well Woman Clinics are an attempt to provide open access so that any woman can go to have a check-up and discuss matters concerning her health with sympathetic health workers.

One of the aims of Well Woman Clinics should also be to reach women who normally do not see their doctor; for example, they may find a male doctor intimidating. Another aim might be to teach women about breast examination and to screen women for cancer of the breast, cervix and ovary. They should raise the consciousness of women about health care. Generally such clinics could train doctors and nurses especially in the concept of self-help and the *prevention* of illness. Unqualified medical staff could be used for this purpose, as in other countries (Gardner 1981: 131–2).

5 Problems in Nursing

One of the main problems of nursing is that there are not enough nurses to go round, according to Mackay (1989: 1). Pay is still under the control of governments determined to limit public expenditure on the NHS. This in turn leads nurses to vote with their feet and they may never return to nursing. This again causes nurses to become an endangered species, with a decrease in the number of young people entering the profession but an increase in the number of elderly people needing nursing care. Nursing is a stressful job, and sometimes nurses do not seem to get respect; for example, doctors may see the nurse as a kind of handmaiden. On the other hand, young people are still coming into the profession for idealistic reasons, and Project 2000, described later, is working towards an all-graduate or diplomate profession.

Other difficulties in the health service include lack of communication and information and the powerlessness felt by many nurses, as Mackay has reported:

Information is power; lack of information is evidence of powerlessness. If you are not told what is going on, you may conclude that you are not deemed of sufficient importance to be told.

For many nurses information was limited to what was going on in their own unit of specialty: 'I know what's going on in the unit but I don't know what's going on in the rest of the hospital.' A staff nurse comments that communication is a particular problem with geographically scattered units, shift working and those who work in relative isolation from colleagues, as in community nursing. Each link in the chain of command is important to good communication. Thus, what information is passed on by nursing officers and sisters affects what and how information is received.

Communication, of course, is a two-way process. Failures of communication also occur when those higher up in the hierarchy get out of touch with those who provide the service. A reduction in the number of nurses may well increase the number of failures of communication as nurses have less and less time to 'walk the job'.

As it was, senior nurses were often felt not to appreciate the efforts of their nursing staff. It is obvious that many nurses work longer hours than they are required to. At the same time many nurses do their utmost to turn up for work. They dislike going off sick yet if they do feel under the weather at work no one notices or suggests they go home. It seems that staffing levels are so tight that interest in nurses' own welfare is supplanted by the more pressing need to keep the wards or unit running (Mackay 1989: 100).

6   The Future of Nursing

Project 2000

In 1987 the United Kingdom Central Council for Nursing, Midwifery and Health Visiting (UKCC) put forward a set of proposals for future nurse training known as Project 2000. After agreement with the government it began to be implemented in stages in the UK between 1989 and 1992. It was proposed that nursing should eventually become an all-graduate profession, with all that that entails, including higher professional status and better education. The following is a summary of some of the main recommendations of Project 2000 for the future of the nursing profession:

● There should be a new registered practitioner competent to assess the need for care.

● There should be a common foundation programme, lasting up to two years.

● Branch programmes should be available, in mental illness, mental handicap, nursing of adults and nursing of children, with experimentation in a branch for midwifery.

● There should be a new, single list of competencies applicable to all registered practitioners at the level of registration and set out in training rules.

● There should be a coherent, comprehensive, cost-effective framework of education beyond registrations.

- There should be specialist practitioners, some of whom will also be team leaders, in all areas of practice in hospital and community settings.

- District nursing, community psychiatric nursing, health visiting and community mental handicap nursing should be specialist qualifications recordable on the UKCC's register.

- There should be a new helper, directly supervised and monitored by a registered practitioner.

- Students should receive training grants which are primarily NHS-controlled.

Community medicine and primary care

The conventional picture of a young person entering nursing, attending nursing school and fulfilling her or his ward duties may be becoming less common (Weir et al. 1988). There are more elderly people now, the standard of living has risen, people have higher expectations, there is a shortage of qualified staff, and technology has developed. All this may lead to more 'care in the community' instead of greater hospital care.

'Primary care' is a term used to refer to the comprehensive care of individuals in the community. It includes treatment by the GP, district nurse, health visitor, voluntary agencies, social services, and so on. Governments have been trying to cut the ever-expanding costs of the health service. The tendency has therefore been to cut the high costs of acute hospital treatment, and expand primary care. Griffiths (1988: 1–2) proposed that local social service authorities (councils, etc.) assess local needs and plan ahead, taking into account the views of those in need.

It could be argued that the people who really lose out are the carers, the relatives of sick or disabled people who now have to be nursed at home, the former hospital in-patients who are now homeless, and so on. The government tries to cut costs and local authorities can't bridge the gap. Many older people have become cynical about the cost of care in the community, which includes the cost of nursing homes provided by the private sector.

7 Towards a Philosophy of Nursing

Perhaps nurses should be encouraged to take an optimistic view by placing the emphasis of a nursing course on health, not on illness. (The Well Woman Clinic is an example of a positive approach.) Maintaining this optimistic view, one aim of Project 2000 should be to prepare the student for further learning – to go on learning: there should be no cut-off point for learning.

Thus the student nurse (and practitioner) should be open to all kinds of learning experience including tending the elderly, following the work of the health visitor and the community nurse, promoting health education, looking at disorders in the community, especially as more people are being (or not being) treated in the community (that is, with a view to improving primary nursing care, for example).

Nurses should look at what people class as health and illness. This may, for example, help nurses to see more clearly the social nature of health and illness, the importance of lay perspectives, their effects on the epidemiology of disease (see the discussion of the social construction of illness in chapter 6).

It seems clear from Project 2000 and the latest medical sociology books that the social sciences will have a bigger role to play in nurse training.

Nurses should know what is meant by the medical model and seek other ways of explaining illness – combining caring with curing.

Finally, nursing should be seen as a full profession. Concepts like professional socialization, professional power and professional ideologies need to be examined to show the nature of professionalism in nursing. This has been the task of this chapter and chapter 2.

8 Conclusions

The subject of this chapter could be analysed by using a number of important concepts in sociology. These concepts are: feminism, sexism, patriarchy, professional ideologies, politicization.

(a) *Feminism.* Historically feminism can be divided into two main periods: the period before the First World War, associated with the women's suffrage movement; and the present period, in which women are seeking a role in government, industry, etc., but also seeking actual power (Banks 1981). However, although society pays lip-service to equal rights for women, the facts, as shown in this chapter and elsewhere, indicate the goals of feminism are still far off. It is the continuing inequalities in pay and power that is one source of discontent in the nursing profession. The struggle continues, and one remedy might be for nurses to become more militant – to become politicized (see later in this section).

(b) *Sexism* means discriminating against a person on account of their sex and implying, for instance, that all women say this or do that. Thus sexism involves labelling the person and predicting their behaviour. It treats the person according to their sex rather than the whole person (in this respect it is somewhat similar to racism, ageism, etc.). There are examples of sexism in this chapter and in chapter 4, such as male doctors who treat female nurses like servants.

(c) *Patriarchy.* This refers to the rule of the family by the father, who seems to make the main decisions in the house. For example, Campbell (1983) says that while improved methods of birth control have freed women from unwanted pregnancy they have not freed women from unwanted sex. Other examples of patriarchy would include the notion that a man had a right to be serviced in the family (the cooking and cleaning being done by his wife), men seeing women as inferior creatures, and so on. There can be an element of patriarchy in the doctor–nurse relationship, at least in cases where the doctor is male and the nurse female. The Well Woman Clinic could provide women with some protection from patriarchy, perhaps by giving practical advice or by offering a counselling service.

(d) *Professional ideologies.* It was suggested in chapter 2 that all professions have beliefs about themselves and that these beliefs often favour the powerful (doctors) against the weaker (nurses and patients). There have been calls for the redomestication of childbirth, to give back to the mother some of the power she had had over her own body.

(e) *Politicization*. This means the coming together of people in a group to fight for their rights. If women were able to do this they would be in a much stronger position today. (See also chapter 2 and Glossary for *politicization*.)

Questions

Self-examination questions

What is meant by the following?

- redomestication of childbirth
- domestic division of labour
- Project 2000
- women's work
- supernumerary

- professional power
- inequalities of women
- patriarchy
- communication

Essay or discussion questions

1 A woman's place is in the home. Discuss.
  Suggestion How far is this an ideology to keep women out of the job market? See Oakley (1976).

2 In what respect has the lot of women in Britain improved in recent years? What are the obstacles to further progress?
  Suggestion Show where reduction in inequalities is not taking place, e.g. the job market, and then seek reasons. Consult the *Employment Gazette* (in most libraries).

3 What would you say are the main causes of frustration in the nursing profession today? How can they be avoided?
  Suggestion See especially Mackay (1989).

4 Attempt a sociology of depression showing
  (a) the contribution sociology can make in this area;
  (b) the unfair treatment of women;

(c)   unnecessary medical intrusion;
(d)   poor conditions at home and work.

Suggestions   Show how sociology can reveal hidden worlds which affect the way in which we see people. (See especially chapters 2 and 6.) Seek the medical definition of depression. See Domanion (1976) and Mitchell (1984).

---

5   Read the extract and answer the question that follows.

Despite the nurse's symbolic encroachment on the space of medical authority, the objective situation of nursing is maintained and her powerlessness preserved. The ritual nature of the complaint system is reminiscent of Goffman's [1968] description of subordinate rituals of rebellion within total institutions which periodically overthrow the hierarchical structure of the asylum at the level of a symbolic critique.

In summary, these complaints have the functions of uniting nurses together as an occupational group with a common experience and language. The complaints de-legitimize the authority structure of the hospital especially with respect to the doctor–nurse relationship, but paradoxically the outcome of this form of complaining is conservative. Because the nurse occupies a subordinate position within the hospi- tal and has little prestige in the market place, she is relatively ineffectual in challenging the structure of the hospital system. Nursing has the traditional weaknesses which are often characteristic of feminized labour, namely the presence of a vicious circle where low job satisfaction results in broken careers and inadequate career structures produce low occupational commitment (from Turner 1987: 154).

Are complaints a threat to the organization?

Suggestion   Complaints may actually strengthen the organization, especially when the complainants as a group are weak (like nurses). The concept of politicization may apply here (see Glossary).

---

6   Read the study and answer the questions at the end.

A review of diabetic care in the primary care setting

Table   *Outcome of studies*

Study	Study	Judgement on results
Wolverhampton	Comparison of patients routinely managed in mini-clinics and those attending a hospital clinic showed no significant differences in three measures of metabolic control. Proportion who default from mini-clinics is considerably smaller than proportion defaulting from hospital.	Mini-clinics achieve the same degree of metabolic control in their diabetic patients as the hospital clinic.
Sheffield	About half the mainly elderly patients discharged were not regularly followed up. Half had high blood sugars, a third signs of peripheral vascular disease and a fifth, both. Two-thirds were pleased to be discharged. A third did not test urine or keep to diet.	Some discharged patients are at risk and need closer supervision.
Tower Hamlets	Thoroughness of clinical review was higher in patients seen in three pilot practices with diabetic support service in patients attending hospital diabetic clinic. Mean glycosylated levels fell significantly in patients seen in pilot practices and did not change in patients attending hospital clinic.	Setting up of pilot diabetic support service is associated with a higher rate of clinical review and improved diabetic control.
Cardiff	Fewer patients in general practice group than in hospital group were regularly reviewed, had regular estimations of blood glucose concentrations and were admitted to hospital for medical reasons. More patients in the general practice group than in the hospital group died. Mean concentrations	Routine care in general practice is less satisfactory than care by the hospital clinic.

Study	Study	Judgement on results
	of HbA_1 higher in general practice group than in the hospital group at end of study.	
Kirkcaldy	No statistically significant differences in selected biochemical or clinical indicators (e.g. symptoms, limb function, fundi, blood pressure, weight, blood sugar and urine analysis). General practice group appeared to include more patients whose control had deteriorated. Number of deaths in general practice group were double those in hospital group. General practice care was half the cost of hospital care for patients and the ambulance service.	No measurable difference in outcomes of people followed up in general practice and in hospital after two years.
Ipswich	One in three discharged patients was not reviewed in two years. Many of those reviewed had no measurement of blood glucose, urine, blood pressure, weight, feet or eye examination.	The standard of supervision in general practice is generally poor and erratic.

Source: J. Wood, Health Trends, vol. 22, no. 9, (1990)

Discussion

Study recommendations.
Five sets of recommendations to improve the delivery of diabetes care in general practice emerged from these studies:
    The need to:

(i)   Maintain computerised district-wide diabetic registers linked with
         a recall and management system which allows self-audit.

(ii)   Provide essential facilities such as diabetic advice, chiropody and rapid access to laboratory and radiographic services for general practitioners.

(iii)   Motivate and keep GPs in touch with current biomedical and educational developments in diabetic care.

(iv)   Involve practice and community nurses more actively in diabetes care.

(v)   Establish close links with the British Diabetic Association to improve patient education.

(a) What does the table show?
(b) Who offers the 'best' treatment?
(c) What policy would you propose?

Suggestions   Discuss the future of 'care in the community'. See Griffiths (1988).

---

7   In the following role-play exercise there are two main characters: the patient, Matthew, and the ward sister, but the cast can be expanded as required – for example, a student nurse, the consultant, and so on. When you have finished the role-play exercise, answer the questions at the end.

Express your views clearly. Be careful to *keep in role*. You could write a brief report of the proceedings afterwards.

Matthew (Matt) Robinson

At 67 you are still a confirmed bachelor, but have a wide circle of friends, and six brothers and sisters younger than yourself with whom you are still very close.

You came into hospital some nine days ago having suffered frequent severe headaches (now 'cured' with painkillers) and a slight weakness of your left hand. The consultant, after lots of seemingly peculiar investigations, has told you that you had a mild stroke, which you will have to learn to live with although 'it shouldn't cause you much trouble and you can go home this weekend and make a return visit to out-patients'. Despite a strong sense of unease, you have tried to carry on as usual, enjoying the company of the other patients and nurses. Recent comments overheard on the doctors' rounds and nurses' reports have alarmed you. You overheard the word 'cancer' one day, although you could not be sure if it referred to you, and everyone seems to treat you as if nothing is wrong. Your attempts to wheedle more information from the nurses have so far met with a cheerful but negative response. Your growing suspicions and sense of frustration that you can't get a 'straight word out of anybody' lead you to ask to have a talk with sister before you go home. You suspect now that death is close to you, but are completely lost as to how you can find out for certain, or if you really want to. By the time the sister arrives your initial resolve has dissipated, the conversation seems set to resolve around the minor details of your discharge.

Nurse

At the age of 27, you have now been a ward sister for almost one year. The ward has acute medical patients, and you have just finished sorting out some of the 'loose ends' at the finish of the consultant's round. The consultant saw one of the patients on his round, Matthew (Matt) Robinson, age 67 and single, with no dependant but a close family group of younger brothers and sisters, and a wide circle of friends. He seems to be a popular man, with the nurses too, always ready with a laugh and a joke, and often helping other patients on the ward.

However, for the past few days, you have noticed that he seems much quieter than usual, and several nurses have commented that he doesn't seem to be his 'usual self', and has started to ask the nurse more probing questions about his illness. He has been told that the weakness in his left hand and recent headaches (he was admitted for investigations – an inoperable cerebral tumour was confirmed) are all due to a mild 'stroke' which will probably not get any worse. After seeing the full results of the test, the consultant told the patient that he had some 'good news' for him this morning, he could go home at the weekend and come back to out-patients in six weeks time. A message from the domestic after the round tells you that Matt wants to have a word with you.

Discussion

A discussion group among a new intake of student nurses, of which only one had previous nursing experience as a nursing auxiliary.

Of the fifteen members of the group:

12 thought more than 50% of the over 65s were in hospital (the actual figure is less than 5%).

10 thought most old people were incontinent.

11 thought more than 50% of over 65s were 'demented'.

All said they would like neither their loved ones nor themselves to be on a 'geriatric' ward.

After a visit to the wards, and a period of discussion in class, all were surprised to learn of the reality – 'they were quite normal to talk to'; 'they didn't smell', etc. (from Wright 1986: 85–8)

(a) How might a nurse analyse the situation?
(b) How might a sociologist analyse the situation?

Further Reading

See Bibliography for full details.

R. Jowell, S. Witherspoon and L. Brook (eds), *British Social Attitudes – the 5th Report* (1988).
L. Mackay, *Nursing a Problem* (1989).
A. Oakley, *Housewife* (1976).
A. Oakley, *Women Confined* (1980).
Project 2000 (1985–7).
J. Salvage, *The Politics of Nursing* (1985).
B. S. Turner, *Medical Power and Social Knowledge* (1987).

There are many books on the feminist perspective; see, for example, other publications by Ann Oakley in the Bibliography.

9 Methods of Research in Sociology for Nurses

1 Introduction

The aim of this chapter is to show the methods used by sociologists in conducting research into *nursing*. The student/researcher should then be able to see more clearly how the research was done and to apply these methods to his/her own research.

Rather than give a long list of dos and don'ts, it may be more useful to show how established researchers went about their task.

The first piece of research studied in this chapter is *The Silent Dialogue* by Olesen and Whittaker (1968). It was chosen because it represents a good example of the method of research known as *participant observation*. In this case study the researchers tried to 'live' among the students as far as possible.

Next the use of the *closed questionnaire* is discussed, and then there are four case studies based on material supplied by student health visitors and district nurses. There then follows a list of the stages in a social survey. Finally, two examples of an interview schedule are given. The chapter concludes with a comparison of different methods of research.

2 Participant Observation

In *The Silent Dialogue* by Olesen and Whittaker (1968), the main method of research was participant observation. The researchers strove to keep in the background as far as possible, yet sought to find out and record everything that happened. Their research was highly intensive; they concentrated their fieldwork on one class, preferring the intensity of this approach to the broader coverage of many classes. They wanted to study in detail such items as the process of socialization, how students confront the faculty on day-to-day matters (such as timetabling, recommended reading), and so on. By seeing students frequently, the researchers believed they could be more sensitive to the students' feelings on such matters as change in themselves and their classmates.

Thus participant observation means, among other things, listening, watching, questioning, understanding, curiosity. The use of an audio-tape recorder is highly recommended, provided of course the interviewees agree. One danger of participant observation is over-empathy with the students.

A comparison with other methods of social research is set out in table 9.3 on pages 152–3.

3 The Closed Questionnaire

The 'Questionnaire for nursing students' inside the box may be taken as an example of a closed questionnaire: a definite reply is requested. Its main advantage is its speed.

A 'neutral' column has been provided for use by respondents when they are really undecided.

The three questions at the end are examples of open questions. They could be answered in writing or told to an interviewer.

This type of questionnaire could be used in market research to estimate the future demand for a product such as hospital equipment, or for this book. It could also be used as a scale to measure how strongly people feel about an issue for example, race.

Questionnaire for nursing students

I am trying to assess the demand for my forthcoming book, *Sociology for Nursing and Health Care*. I should be grateful if you would kindly complete this form by ticking the appropriate columns.

	Strongly agree	Agree	Neutral	Disagree	Strongly disagree
I find most sociology books and articles quite interesting					
I find most sociology books and articles difficult to understand					
I find most sociology books and articles enlightening					
I find sociology books useful in my work					
I have borrowed sociology books from the library					
I have bought just one sociology book in the last 12 months					
I have bought two or more sociology books in the last year					

Open questions

How can sociology books be improved?

How can sociology be improved?

What improvements (if any) would you suggest for your course?

4   Four Case Studies

The following studies were based on material supplied by student health visitors and district nurses. They could be taken as further examples of participant observation methods of research. The data were collected through conversation with the interviewees. These studies should be of interest to students in health visiting and district nursing as well as those in general and psychiatric nursing.

Case study 1

Mrs L   was expecting her first baby. She was particularly nervous about the labour.

Her mother-in-law was a 'matter-of-fact', 'sensible' woman.

Mrs L had other, more general fears. She was afraid that she was not fulfilling the ideals society expected of her – i.e. not to be frightened, to be reliable and to be able to cope. This only made her more apprehensive because she *was* frightened.

Her father was a 'Victorian authoritarian' figure.

When the baby was born, she complained about small things and was generally over-protective. She was depressed and off sex. She also became more demanding. Finally she said she did not feel 'maternal'. This made her feel worse because she thought 'you were supposed to feel maternal'.

Assignment   Attempt a sociological account of what is happening, referring particularly to society's expectations, the use of 'good' words and 'bad' words, and the social causes of fears and depressions (see Mitchell 1984).

Comments   'Good' words might include 'coping' and 'maternal', for example. See C. Wright Mills (1970) and chapter 1 for private troubles and public issues.

Case study 2

Mrs J   is an old lady. She lives with her son and family. She could look after herself (according to the health visitor) but 'has given up'. She seems to make herself awkward. It would be difficult to find a suitable 'home' for her even assuming the rest of the family wanted this.

Assignment   What comments would you make on the assumption that in the family we look after one another (or should do)?

What comments would you make on the assumption that the welfare state will look after us?

What do you feel causes the 'mother-in-law' problem?

What difference would it made if Mrs J's adult child was a daughter?

Comments   The predicaments of this family are connected with the housing shortage; the myth of 'care in the community' (often this is insufficient); the expectation that the adult daughter will look after the whole family.

Case study 3

Mrs W   is a working-class mother whose baby is now a few months old. She was pregnant before the marriage. The couple now live in a one-bedroom flat. Mrs W is quite young. There is a close-knit family network.

The health visitor noticed that the mother was giving the baby solids too early. When this was mentioned Mrs W said she did this so that the husband (who is a shift-worker) could have a good night's sleep. Mrs W had consulted her mother and her neighbours, who all confirmed that they had given their babies solids at an early age. The grandmother wanted a 'chubby' baby – 'Feed the boy and make him a strong man,' she said.

The father's participation in family affairs was low, and Mrs W felt it was her responsibility to ensure her husband got a good night's sleep and that the family ran smoothly.

Assignment   Give a sociological account of what is happening here. What is the 'role' of Mrs W with respect to the other 'actors'? Where does her role come from? Who is her 'audience'? What is a good or poor 'performance'?

Comments   Sexism and patriarchy seem to pervade this family (see chapter 8). Family can also act as a sort of prison (see, for example, Gavron 1983). Use Goffman (1969).

Case study 4

Mr and Mrs A   are a couple in their early twenties. They have a boy of three and a girl of six months.

   Mr A is a manual worker, is bored with his job and drinks heavily.

   The family have money problems and their spending seems to be injudicious; for example, they recently bought a video camera.

   There are not many toys around the house. The boy's speech is poorly developed.

   Mrs A married young, the man being like her father. She now feels 'trapped'.

   She gave up breast-feeding the baby after three months but did not tell the health visitor.

Assignment   Attempt a sociological analysis concentrating on 'patterns' of behaviour – i.e. how this pattern is repeated elsewhere in society, what are the effects of inequality in society, etc.?

Comment   See chapter 5.

Other assignments

Please also produce case study examples of actual conversations; the analysis of political, industrial and social events in the news; a sociological analysis of your course, etc. That is to say, widen the focus.

5   Stages in a Social Survey

The following extract shows the stages in a social survey. There are no rigid rules for this: adapt your survey to suit the circumstances.

1 Choice of topic to be studied.
2 Forming of hunches and hypotheses.
3 Identification of the population to be surveyed.
4 Carrying out preparatory investigations and interviews.
5 Drafting the questionnaire or interview schedule.
6 Conducting a pilot survey.
7 Finalizing the questionnaire.
8 Selecting a sample of the population.
9 Selection and training of interviewers (if necessary).
10 Collecting the data.
11 Processing the data and analysing the results.
12 Writing the research report, perhaps in the form of a book.

(McNeill 1985: 17)

6 Interview Schedules

Questionnaire for intensive interviews

The following extract shows the questionnaire used in one of the best-known pieces of research since the Second World War, *Family and Kinship in East London* by Young and Willmott (1957).

Interview Schedule – Bethnal Green Marriage Sample

(Unless otherwise stated, the questions could be answered by either husband or wife)

1 How long have you lived here (present home)?
2 How did you get this place? (Recommended by relatives? Inherited from relatives?)
3 Where did you live straight after you got married? (With relatives? which?)
4 *Ask both husband and wife.* Do you want to move out of Bethnal Green?

5 *Ask both husband and wife.* What do you think of Bethnal Green?

6 *Ask wife.* Are you working? (Part-time, full-time, outwork?) If working outside home, who looks after the children?

7 Have you any friends that visit in their homes more often than once a month? Have you any friends who visit you here more than once a month? (List for husband and wife – each friend and how often visiting or visited.)

8 Was . . . (youngest child) born at home or in hospital? Were you (wife) churched afterwards?

9 (At last confinement.) Did other child(ren) go away? If so, to whom? If not, who looked after them?

10 Did anyone else help during or just after confinement with: shopping, cleaning, cooking, washing?

11 *Ask wife.* When you were last ill in bed, who helped with the home and children?

12 *Ask wife.* Can you give me an idea of what a typical day is like for you – when you go out, who you see, who calls here, who you visit and so on?

13 Do you/does your husband help with housework? For example, when did you/he last do the washing up?

14 *Ask wife.* When you go out in the evenings, who looks after the children?

15 Now I want to ask about family gatherings. Can you tell me whether your family meets at Christmas or on other regular occasions? Can you recall any recent gatherings which relatives came to?

16 Who came to your wedding? (Record adult kin on kinship diagram.)

17 Where were the wedding and reception? Who paid for the wedding and reception?

18 How and where did you first meet each other?

19 During courtship, whose home were you at most often?

20 Were your children christened? If so, who were the god-parents? (List godparents.)

(Young and Willmott 1957: 196–7)

One of the main conclusions of this study was that there was a strong link between the married daughter and the mother. The daughter visited her mother several times a week. The link was especially strong in working-class families.

An example of methods used in a large-scale survey

The survey examined here is J. and E. Newson's *Patterns of Infant Care in an Urban Community* (1965), which was based on 700 mothers in the Nottingham area and their one-year-old babies. Its main purpose was to show how babies were brought up in England. Other aims included an investigation into class differences in infant care and examination of the relationship between expectant mothers and health visitors. Tables 9.1 and 9.2 show some of the findings from this and the Newsons' later study, *Four Year Old in an Urban Community* (1970). Then part of the questionnaire used in the 1965 survey is reproduced.

Table 9.1   Class differences in the care of children from birth to 12 months

	Social classes I and II[a] (%)	Social class V[b] (%)
Still breast-feeding at 1 month	60	34
Dummy given at some time	39	74
Normal bedtime before 6.30 p.m.	47	31
Child sleeps in own room	54	3
Diet judged inadequate in protein or vitamin C	5	32
Mother checks genital play	25	93
Generally smacks the child for offences	39	58
High participation in child care by father	57	36
Couple seldom go out together	25	59
Mother's age 21 or less at first birth	24	53

[a]Social classes I and II = professional and managerial.
[b]Social class V = unskilled manual.
Source: Newson and Newson (1965)

Table 9.2   Class differences in the care of children at four years old

	Social classes I and II (%)	Social class V (%)
One child only (at time of interview)	17	1
Mother's age 27 or less	9	27
Strong desire for quiet, neatness and cleanliness	3	10
Mother participates in children's play	71	45
Mother/father regularly reads bedtime stories	56	14
Mother gives false information 'where do babies come from?'	8	66
Punitive response to bedwetting	10	88

Source: Newson and Newson (1970)

Other general findings suggested that working-class parents married younger, had more children and had fewer material advantages (the child was unlikely to have a room of its own). The researchers considered that middle-class mothers had a 'better attitude' to pregnancy; for example, they attended antenatal classes more regularly.

Part of the questionnaire used in this research is reproduced here. The first section alone reveals some interesting information, such as the date of birth of the baby, the mother's age and the size of the family. This sort of information may be of interest to the health visitor and the sociologist.

The Questionnaire

University of Nottingham
Child Health Research Unit

Clinic District ....

Interviewer ....

Date ....

GUIDED INTERVIEW SCHEDULE
(for mothers of children aged 1:0)
Where alternative answers are shown the appropriate answer should
be *underlined*.

1. Orientation data

Child's full name ....

Address ....
....

Date of birth ....   Sex: Boy/Girl

Family size and position (for each child), indicate sex, age and whether
foster (F), deceased (D), or stillbirth (S)

ELDEST

Sex

Age

Foster, dec'd,
stillbirth

Additional notes (give dates of any deaths, stillbirths or miscarriages)
....
....

Mother: Age ......   Not working/working part-time/full-time
Occupation if at work...............................
If working: Who looks after the baby?
....

Father: Age ......   Precise occupation.......................................
Does he have to be away from home except during
the day?
Home every night/up to 2 nights away/more than
2 nights away/normally away/separation or di-
vorce/dead/other (specify below, e.g. night shift)
....
....

2.   Birth data

Place: Home/other (give name) ....
Birth weight ....
How did you get on? Did you have a good time?
(note how spontaneous comments reveal mother's attitude)
....
....
....

Assessment of mother's attitude: (tick on appropriate line)
..... Positive (enjoyed birth, interesting experience)
..... Not very positive (not too bad, all right, could have been worse)
..... Negative (unpleasant, distasteful, had a bad time)
..... Impossible to assess

Was it a normal birth? Prolonged labour/induced/Caesarean/breech/
birth injury/other?
....

Prompt: Premature/late? ...... days. Stitches? ....

Were you conscious at the moment the baby was born?
YES/NO

Was anyone present at the birth, apart from the doctor, midwife or
nurse? ....

How soon were you out of bed for the whole day? ....

Did you do any special exercise during your pregnancy?
YES/NO

If YES, specify for how long, and on whose advice? ....
....

Did you have any help in the house after the baby was born?
Husband at home all day/relative/neighbour/friend/local authority
home help/private help/other ....
For how long? ....

If other than husband, specify whether living in: YES/NO
Do you normally have any help in the house? (specify how often,
and whether paid) ....

Has the baby ever been separated from you? YES/NO
Details ....
....

At what age? .... For how long? ....

3. Feeding

History

<table>
<tr><th></th><th colspan="14">Age in months</th></tr>
<tr><th></th><th>0</th><th>1</th><th>2</th><th>3</th><th>4</th><th>5</th><th>6</th><th>7</th><th>8</th><th>9</th><th>10</th><th>11</th><th>12</th><th>13</th></tr>
<tr><td>Breast</td><td></td><td></td><td></td><td></td><td></td><td></td><td></td><td></td><td></td><td></td><td></td><td></td><td></td><td></td></tr>
<tr><td>Bottle</td><td></td><td></td><td></td><td></td><td></td><td></td><td></td><td></td><td></td><td></td><td></td><td></td><td></td><td></td></tr>
<tr><td>Solid</td><td></td><td></td><td></td><td></td><td></td><td></td><td></td><td></td><td></td><td></td><td></td><td></td><td></td><td></td></tr>
</table>

Remarks: ....
....

Breast feeding
If little or no breast feeding: Did you have any special reason for not breast feeding? ....

....

If any breast feeding: Did you enjoy feeding the baby?

....

Did you have any difficulties? ....

....

If stopped, how? Sudden/gradual
Did you have any special reason for stopping when you did? ....
On doctor's advice? ....
Did the baby mind? ....

....

Bottle feeding
Any special difficulties? ....

....

If stopped, how? Sudden/gradual ....
Any special reason? ....

....

Did the baby mind? ....

....

Ask all mothers: Does the baby use a bottle at all now? (e.g. for orange juice) ....

Feeding schedule: Rigid to clock/flexibly rigid/flexible/demand
(Specimen question: if the baby was asleep, did you wake him for his feed? If he cried before the normal time, did you feed him? What did you do if he didn't seem hungry? How long did you allow the feed to continue?)

N.B. The point to look for is whether the routine was decided by the baby or the mother: thus, if baby was fed when he liked, and this happened to be regularly every four hours, 'demand' should be marked.

Sources of advice on feeding schedule: Doctor/midwife/H.V./hospital/ baby's grandmother/relative/friend/own experience/lectures/magazines/books/other ....

Did you get advice from books or magazines? Specify titles: ....
....

Present solid feeding
Previous day's meals. What did he have to eat yesterday? (Specify in detail what food was offered to the child, even if it was not in fact eaten)
Breakfast ....
....
Dinner ....
....
Tea ....
....
Any other meal? ....

Did he have anything between meals? (prompt)
                              Sweets? .... Fruit? ....
                              Ice cream? .... Biscuits ....
(indicate how much)   Other? ....

About how much milk does he drink altogether? ....
Any other drinks? ....
Does he have Welfare orange juice? YES/NO
Cod-liver oil? YES/NO
Note any substitutes for either of these by name ....
....
Are there any foods he won't take? ....
....
What do you do when you prepare something for him and he won't eat it? (full details) ....
....
(If mother says this never happens, say 'What would you do?')

Assessment of mother's attitude (tick on appropriate line)
...... Anxious (battles, much coaxing, persuasion for every mouthful)
...... Mildly concerned (much encouragement)
...... Unconcerned (takes no notice, lets child leave it)

Present non-nutritive suckling behaviour
Objects habitually sucked (prompt): Fingers/thumbs/hands/or ring/ EMPTY bottle/cloth/dummy/ ....

How much? Continually/frequently/occasionally/not at all
Does he have any special time when he sucks things?
When sleepy/when hungry/when thwarted/other ....
....
Have you tried to stop it at all? YES/NO
If yes: How? ....
....
Did he mind? ....
Has he ever had a dummy? YES/NO
If mother disapproves of dummies, in words or by tone of voice, tick
here ...... (DO NOT PROMPT THIS)

Assessment of mother's attitude: (tick appropriate line)
......   Intolerant (prolonged restraint, or attempts thereat)
......   Semi-permissive (discouragement, mildly dissuasive)
......   Permissive (ignores or encourages habit)

4.   **Sleeping habits**

Sleep pattern during previous day and night

What time was he put to bed last night? ....
How soon after that did he go to sleep? ....
Did he wake during the night? YES/NO
If YES: at what time(s)? ....
How long did he stay awake? ....
What time did he wake up this morning? ....
What time did he get up this morning? ....
If more than a quarter hour's difference between these two times,
ask: What did he do between those times? ....
....
Did he have a daytime rest yesterday? YES/NO
At what time(s)?   From .... to .... (A.M.)
                         From .... to .... (P.M.)
How long did he actually sleep in the daytime?
                         A.M. .... P.M. ....

7 Conclusions

The various methods of sociological research described in this chapter are compared in table 9.3.

Finally there is one further distinction made in sociology: it is the difference between positive or scientific sociology and interpretative sociology. The former seeks to explain what is going on in a law-like, provable way, whereas the latter tries to *understand* what is going on. The former relies on closed questionnaires, while the latter relies more on open questions and in-depth interviews.

Questions

Self-examination questions

What is meant by the following?

- participant observation
- closed questionnaire
- open question
- private trouble
- public issue
- patterns of infant care
- guided interview schedule

Essay or discussion questions

1 When might you use: a closed questionnaire; an open questionnaire; participant observation?
  Suggestion See table 9.3.

2 Is there any particular research you would like to carry out in your hospital (or establishment)? Give details.

Table 9.3 Types of research methods

Type of methodology	Brief description	Advantages	Disadvantage
1 Participant observation	Becoming part of the group you are studying.	The researcher can get to know what group members are really thinking, saying and doing in a way which is not possible using formal questionnaires.	(a) There is a danger of becoming too sympathetic to the group you are studying. (b) The results cannot be checked.
2 Experimental method	Comparing an experimental group with a control group.	The researcher can obtain scientifically testable results.	Cannot really be used in sociological research (though it is frequently used by psychologists in controlled experiments).
3 Informal or unstructured interview	The researcher has a rough idea of what he or she wants to ask and encourages interviewees to talk.	Useful for ideas. Interviewees may say many things that the researcher has not thought of.	The results cannot be tested.

4	Diaries	Respondents are asked to keep a diary.	Encourages respondents to record in a methodical way what happens to them.	It depends on the respondent's diligence.
5	Formal questionnaires with open questions	The interviewer asks set questions. Interviewees reply in their own words.	Covers the research in a methodical way. The interviewees' replies can be coded and quantified.	It is difficult to really test the deeper feelings. How strongly do respondents really feel on these questions?
6	Formal questionnaires with closed questions	The interviewee may, for example, be asked to tick appropriate boxes or just give 'yes' or 'no' answers.	The answers are definite and can be measured mathematically. This type of questionnaire can be used in surveys.	As above. The questions must be clear and precise.

Source: Joseph (1990)

Further Reading

See Bibliography for full details.

J. M. Clark and L. Hockey, *Further Research for Nursing* (1989).
E. Goffman, *The Presentation of Self in Everyday Life* (1969).
P. E. Hammond (ed.), *Sociologists at Work* (1964).
I. C. Henry and G. Pashley, *Health Care Research* (1990).
M. Joseph, *Sociology for Everyone* (1990).
P. McNeill, *Research Methods* (1985).
P. H. Mann, *Methods of Sociological Enquiry* (1976).

10   Conclusions

It is possible to have two sets of conclusions to this study, one from the viewpoint of the sociologist and one from the viewpoint of the nurse.

1 The Sociological Viewpoint

The sociologist may see this topic as part of general sociology and use similar concepts to investigate other aspects of society. For example, sociology can be used as a tool to investigate the process of change from student to nurse, from layperson to professional. But the concept of sociology can also be used to study other changes, for example the transition from immigrant to citizen, from officer cadet to officer, from girl to woman, and so on.

Another useful concept is power. The exercise of power in hospitals is similar to that in other large organizations and helps the sociologist to expose hidden organizational ideologies. There are also the concepts of profession socialization and total institution as described in the text.

Berger invites us to take the unofficial view of what is going on and look at society from different viewpoints. Thus in a hospital committee meeting there may be several people, each with a different view. Often sociologists would look at the meeting from the viewpoint of the least powerful because this view may be least recognized; sociologists may also look for the latent function of organization. For all these tasks Mills (1970) advises us to develop the sociological imagination. We should look not just at the individual but also at the socialized member of society. It is not a biological or psychological account we are seeking but rather a sociological one.

An important theme of sociology is inequality, and it is part of the sociologist's task to reveal it, whether it is inequality in class, race, gender or health (although some sociologists have argued that society needs some inequality in order to give individuals a chance to aspire to the higher levels of society) (Segalman and Marsland 1989).

2   The Nursing Viewpoint

Following from the sociological view, we may say that all is not what it seems, that we should question everything including everyday common sense, the obvious and the hidden.

Remember the importance of socialization along with prior socialization and anticipatory socialization. Decisions may be made based on socialization which occurred many years ago. Consider Merton's study *The Student Physician* (1957), where the student's socialization was seen to last a lifetime.

For many students the inequalities of health are greater than they thought. However, students should not be partisan. Detect the inequalities in health, say, but do not make hasty judgements.

Know how the hospital or other establishment works; understand the professional ideologies, the managerial ideologies, the interaction of managers and doctors, the reasons for poor communications in hospitals. The various parties (doctors, nurses, etc.) have had different socialization and this *perhaps* makes them insensitive to other viewpoints.

Nurses get a bad deal in many ways; this reflects the unequal treatment of women, given the fact that the majority of nurses are women. Often pay and conditions are poor, their professionalism is unrecognized, they work in rigid hierarchies, there are many petty annoyances, and they are often required to do menial work. Project

2000 aims to make nursing an all-graduate profession, and this may help to overcome some of the difficulties.

Overall sociology will give nurses a clearer insight into society and their place in it. It is a controversial subject, but that might be a good thing. What do you think?

Glossary

(After consulting the Glossary, see Index for further details.)

Ageism Distinguishing against a person on account of his or her age (and implying 'all older people do this').

Class In Western societies class is usually defined on the basis of occupation. Thus the highest classes are in the highest occupations (such as professional and managerial), while the lowest class would be in the lowest occupations (unskilled manual).

Clinical freedom Studies show clinicians want full freedom in the way they practise medicine in hospitals, etc. They do not necessarily demand a say in the management of the organization.

Culture See *Norms and values*.

Deviant subculture A group of people sharing similar beliefs and ideologies which usually sees itself as contesting the remainder of society. Deviant subcultures may be found in schools, in criminal deviant subculture, on the drug scene, etc. (See Becker 1963).

Dual labour markets In most societies there may be at least two sub-markets for labour. The primary market comprises the best jobs and the secondary market contains the low-paid, low-skilled, nonunionized jobs. Such workers are trapped in the secondary labour market. Usually they are women. (See also *Reserve army of labour*.)

Feminism A social movement seeking equal rights for women through equal opportunity at work and the abolition of patriarchy and sexism. Early feminists sought equal rights within the existing 'system', particularly the right to vote. Later, in the sixties, feminism became a mass movement strongly advocating equality. One difficulty for feminists is that because married women with children are more tied to their own families they do not come together as a strong movement, i.e. they do not become politicized and so they 'grieve' in private (see Gavron 1983), rather than assert their right to a full life based on equality. (See also Mills (1970) for the link between private troubles and public issues. What appears to be a purely personal problem is in fact a public issue, for example discrimination against women in the job market.)

Gender 'Sex' refers to the obvious biological difference between men and women, whereas 'gender' refers to the social and cultural difference. Thus the role of a woman varies from society to society, and the example often given is the comparison of women in Islamic societies with those from Western societies. There is an enormous amount of feminist literature illustrating gender, sexism and patriarchy, etc. (See also *Role*.)

Ideology A set of beliefs about the social world. These beliefs may be distorted and not based on actual facts. Often these beliefs are used to justify the position of powerful people in society, for example the power of men over women (sexism), whites over blacks (racism), and so on (see chapter 2). This working definition of ideology has been used in this book to analyse the social world, for example, 'scientific management', 'patriarchy' and 'fascism', etc.

Further characteristics of an ideology are:

1 The beliefs and values comprising these ideologies form a set, that is to say, they are interconnected.

2 Ideologies are determined by the economic arrangements of society; hence many believe the owners of the means of production (the bourgeoisie) influence or control the ideas of society (see chapter 5).

3   Ideologies are linked to the sociology of knowledge. What passes for knowledge is socially determined.

4   Karl Mannheim believed ideologies could either maintain the status quo or promote social change – hence the title of his book *Ideology and Utopia* (1991). Anthony Giddens (1989) shows how ideologies can be used to justify force. For example, intruders can justify their activities by seeing themselves as 'civilizing' the 'heathen' peoples with whom they come into contact.

Individualism   Stresses the importance of the individual against institutions, especially the state (Segalman and Marsland 1989).

Medical model   Treating sick individuals as if they were machines that needed repair rather than as people in their own right (Kennedy 1981). Having a 'scientific' approach to medicine at the expense of other possible approaches, for example preventative medicine.

Norms and values   Values may denote the cultural beliefs in a society; norms are the ways of achieving them. The culture of a society consists of its norms and values. Alternatively, it could refer to everything that that society produces. Thus in most Western societies people seek financial success and see hard work as the means of achieving success. The same may be true of professions to some extent.

Nursing process   Nurse and patient act as a team to solve the patient's problem. It involves four stages: assessment of patient's problems; planning how to resolve them; implementation of the plans; and evaluation of their success (*Mini Dictionary for Nurses* 1991).

Patriarchy   The dominance of the male in the family, including the control of finance and sexual demands by the male head of the household.

Pluralism   Assumes society is composed of a wide variety of competing groups – economic, professional, religious, etc. The government does not interfere except to ensure that everyone keeps to the rules and that rights of individuals are upheld.

Polarization   A coming-together of those with similar class interests against those with opposing interests.

Politicization A growing awareness of your class position through association with others (see also *Feminism* above).

Power The probability that a person can carry out his or her will.

Prejudice Literally pre-judgement using stereotypes. In racial prejudice, for example, there is an assumption that all black people will behave in a certain way. 'Discrimination' means actually acting according to your prejudice.

Professional ideologies Most professions – medicine, law, accountancy – have beliefs about their work. Some sociologists believe that the medical profession has a 'cure' ideology. It overemphasizes 'cures' rather than preventative medicine or making improvements in social conditions, for example reducing poverty in society, etc. (See Kennedy 1981).

Qualitative data Includes conversations, participant observation, letters, diaries, etc. See case studies towards the end of chapter 9.

Quantitative data Facts and figures, e.g. the relationship between unemployment and suicide.

Racism Discrimination on the basis of a person's race. Beliefs about people's race determine attitudes towards them. (See also *Prejudice, Dual labour markets, Reserve army of labour.*)

Reserve army of labour This is the part of the labour force that is taken on in good times only and is the first to be laid off in hard times. In most societies the reserve army includes unskilled workers, women, racial minorities and the elderly.

Response rate What proportion of people taking part in a study actually fill in a questionnaire, or return a completed questionnaire in the post. Thus, for example, out of say 100 persons required to return a questionnaire only 70 may do so. This is a response rate of 70 per cent.

Role Role is the behaviour expected of us. Obvious examples are the role of man, woman, mother, father, teacher, nurse, accountant. Sociologists see role mainly as learned behaviour rather than biologically determined behaviour. Some people learn their roles better than others; few are clumsy. Societies differ in the ways these roles are performed. Goffman uses the analogy with the theatre to explain the concept of role. Thus society writes the script but the individual plays the part written. The individual is given the part and may perform it well – or not so well. (See Goffman 1969.)

Role conflict   Performing two or more inconsistent roles. For example, a teacher is marking the exam paper of his or her child who is also his or her pupil (the role of parent conflicts with the role of an impartial teacher). Another example of role conflict is a factory supervisor who is also the safety officer. He or she may wish to raise production but in doing so may overlook hazards at work – the roles of production officer and safety officer conflict.

Sample   A group of people selected for study. A random sample is where the group members are selected at random, for example, every tenth member of the class. Sociologists prefer a random sample as it enables them to make general statements about the whole group; for example, from a random sample of 3000, researchers can try to forecast the behaviour of the population of Britain as a whole (having a population of about 60 million).

Scientific management   This holds that management has the full right to manage and that management can say not only what is to be done but how it is to be done. Management's control of the task was systematically analysed by Frederick Taylor in his book *The Principles of Scientific Management*, first published in 1911. Scientific management is seen by many sociologists (Braverman, etc.) as an ideology justifying over-zealous control by management. This is a frequent cause of bad industrial relations. It can apply to hospitals too.

Sexism   Discrimination against men and women on account of their gender; for example, the belief that women can only do certain kinds of work, a belief in male dominance (see also *Gender*, *Patriarchy*).

Sick role   Here the sick individual is permitted to withdraw from the 'world'. The doctor has the right to apply skills and examine the patient. (Chapter 4 and Parsons 1951.)

Social construction of reality   The process by which people create a personal view of social reality as they are socialized into society. This subjective view of reality becomes objectified as social institutions, that is to say regular shared patterns of behaviour. (See *Role, Socialization*, Berger and Luckman 1984.)

Social mobility   Moving up or down in social class is often defined in terms of one's occupation; an example of upward social mobility would be a labourer becoming a clerk. Sociologists are interested in social mobility rates as they indicate how open a society is. Thus a high rate of social mobility would indicate an open society in which people from humble positions can rise to higher positions. Intergenerational mobility compares the positions achieved by an individual during the course of his or her life.

Socialization   Acquiring the norms and values of the society of which the individual is a member. It usually involves transition to a higher stage, for example, from girl to woman, from woman to nurse, from immigrant to citizen, from medical student to doctor. Associated terms: prior socialization, anticipatory socialization, primary socialization (first few years of life), secondary socialization, professional socialization. (See *Norms and values*; Becker et al. 1961; Olesen and Whittaker 1968.)

Stigma   We may concentrate on the person's stigma first rather than accept the whole person, for example, we may concentrate on the person being black rather than see the man or woman as a whole person first (racism). Sometimes we may react with repulsion or overhearty acceptance (Goffman 1990).

Total institution   A term used by Goffman to describe organizations which try completely to control their members. Such organizations may include prisons, secure hospitals, military academies, religious communities, etc. They define the life their inmates are to live.

Universalism (in welfare)   The view that individuals should be treated equally regardless of means (Marshall 1963).

Bibliography

Abercrombie, N. et al. (1984) *Penguin Dictionary of Sociology.* Penguin, Harmondsworth.

Allen, M. (1983) *Primary Care Nursing: Research Care Nursing in Action.* In L. Hockey, *Primary Care Nursing.* Churchill Livingstone, London.

Armstrong, D. (1983a). 'The Fabrication of Nurse/Patient Relationships'. *Social Science and Medicine*, 17: 457–60.

Armstrong, D. (1983b) *An Outline of Sociology as Applied to Medicine.* Wright, Bristol.

Baly, M. E. (ed.) (1981) *A New Approach to District Nursing.* Heinemann, London.

Banks, O. (1981) *Faces of Feminism.* Martin Robertson, Oxford.

Becker, H. (1963) *Outsiders.* Free Press, New York.

Becker, H. et al. (1961) *Boys in White.* University of Chicago Press, Chicago.

Behan, B. (1964) *Borstal Boy.* Corgi, London.

Bendix, R. (1959) *Max Weber: An Intellectual Portrait.* Methuen, London.

Berger, P. (1966) *Invitation to Sociology.* Penguin, Harmondsworth.

Berger, P. and Luckman, T. (1984) *The Social Construction of Reality.* Penguin, Harmondsworth.

Bernstein, B. (1964) *Class Codes and Controls*, Vol. 2. Routledge & Kegan Paul, London.

Bilton, T. et al. (1987) *Introductory Sociology.* 2nd edn. Macmillan, London.

Blaxter, M. (1990) *Health and Lifestyles*. Tavistock/Routledge, London.

Blaxter, M. and Paterson, E. (1982) *Mothers and Daughters: A Three-Generational Study of Health Attitudes and Behaviour*. Heinemann, London.

Bloor, M. (1976). 'Professional Autonomy and Client Exclusion. A Study in ENT Clinics'. In *Studies in Everyday Medical Life*, ed. M. Wadsworth and D. Robinson. Martin Robertson, London.

Bodenheimer, T. (1990) 'Should We Abolish the Private Health Insurance Industry?' *International Journal of Health Services*, 20 (2), 199–220.

Bond, J. and Bond, S. (1986) *Sociology and Health Care*. Longman, London.

Braverman, H. (1974) *Labour and Monopoly Capital*. Monthly Review Press, New York.

Brendan, B. (1992) 'A Scalpel for the Red Tape'. *The Health Service Journal*, 5 March.

Britten, N. (1986) 'Hospital Consultants' View of their Patients'. *Sociology of Health and Illness*, 13 (1), 83–97.

Brown, G. W. (1984) 'Depression – A Sociological View'. In N. Black et al., *Health and Disease: A Reader*. Open University Press, Milton Keynes, pp. 76–82.

Calman, M. and Johnson, B. (1985) 'Health, Health Risks and Inequalities'. *Sociology of Health and Illness*, 17.

Campbell, B. (1983) 'Sex: A Family Affair'. In L. Segal (ed.), *What is to be Done about the Family*. Penguin, Harmondsworth.

Cartwright, A. (1967) *Patients and Doctors*. Routledge & Kegan Paul, London.

Cavanagh, S. I. (1991) 'The Conflict Management Style of Staff Nurses and Nurse Managers'. *Journal of Advanced Nursing*, 16, 1254–60.

Clark, J. M. and Hockey, L. (1989) *Further Research for Nursing*. Scutari Press, London.

Clay, T. (1987) *Nurses: Power and Politics*. Heinemann, London.

Cockerham, W. C. (1987) *Medical Sociology*. Prentice-Hall, Englewood Cliffs, NJ.

Cooper, D. (1971) *The Death of the Family*. Penguin, Harmondsworth.

Copperman, H. (1983) *Dying at Home*. Wiley, Chichester.

Coser, L. A. (1956) *The Function of Social Conflict*. Free Press, Glencoe.

Cox, D. (1991) 'Health Service Management – A Sociological View: Griffith and the Non-negotiated Order of the Hospital'. In Gabe et al. (1991).

Dahrendorf, R. (1959) *Class and Class Conflict in Industrial Society*. Stanford University Press, Stanford.

Dalley, G. (1988) *Ideologies of Caring*. Macmillan, London.

Davis, B. (1983) 'Model Student'. *Nursing Mirror*, 157 (21), 40–1.

Davis, F. (1960) 'Uncertainty in Medical Diagnosis – Chemical and Functional'. *American Journal of Sociology*, 66, 44–7.

Davis, M. (1963) *Passage Through Crisis – Polio Victims and Their Families*. Bobbs-Merrill, Indianapolis.

Dewing, J. (1990) 'Reflective Practice'. *Seminar Nurse*, 4 (3).

DHSS (Department of Health and Social Security) (1983) *NHS Management Enquiry: The Griffiths Report*, DHSS, HMSO, London.

Disken, S. (1990) 'A Role for Doctors on the Management Scene'. *The Health Service Journal*, 1 March, p. 321.

Domanion, J. (1976) *Depression*. Fontana, Glasgow.

Durkheim, E. (1952) *Suicide*. Routledge & Kegan Paul, London.

Ehrenreich, B. and English, D. (1974) 'Complaints and Disorders'. *The Sexual Politics of Sickness*. Compendum, London.

Epstein, S. S. (1990) 'Losing the War against Cancer'. *International Journal of Health Services*, 10 (1).

Etzioni, A. (1961) *Written Organizations*. Free Press, Glencoe.

Etzioni, A. (ed.) (1969) *The Semi-Professions and their Organization*. Free Press, New York.

Fallowfield, L. (1990) *The Quality of Life: The Missing Measurement in Health Care*. Souvenir Press, London.

Fitzpatrick, R. (1982) *The Experience of Illness*. Tavistock, London.

Foucault, M. (1973) *The Birth of the Clinic*. Tavistock, London.

Freidson, E. (1986) *Professional Powers*. University of Chicago Press, Chicago.

Friedman, M. and Rosenman, R. H. (1974) *Type A Behaviour and Your Heart*. Knopf, New York.

Gabe, J., Calnan, M. and Bury, M. (eds) (1991) *The Sociology of the Health Service*. Routledge, London.

Gamlin, R. (1989) 'What do you Mean Sister?' *Senior Nurse*, 19 (6) (June).

Gardner, K. (1981) 'Well Woman Clinics: A Positive Approach to Women's Health'. In H. Roberts (ed.), *Women, Health and Reproduction*. Routledge & Kegan Paul, London.

Gavron, H. (1983) *The Captive Wife*. Routledge, London.

Gerth, H. H. and Mills, C. Wright (eds) ([1948] 1991) *From Max Weber: Essays in Sociology*. Routledge, London.

Giddens, A. (1989) *Sociology*. Polity Press, Cambridge.

Goffman, E. (1968) *Asylums*. Penguin, Harmondsworth.

Goffman, E. (1969) *The Presentation of Self in Everyday Life*. Penguin, Harmondsworth.

Goffman, E. (1990) *Stigma*. Penguin, London.

Gordon, R. (1957) 'Mortality Experience among the Japanese in the United States, Hawaii and Japan'. *Public Health Reports*, 72, 550. Repr. in Tuckett (1976).

Gordon, R. (1967) 'Further Experience among Japanese Americans'. *Public Health Reports*, 82, 973–4. Repr. in Tuckett (1976).

Griffiths, R. (1988) *Community Care: Agenda for Action*. HMSO, London.

Halmoss, P. (1970) *The Personal Service Society*. Constable, London.

Hammond, P. E. (ed.) (1964) *Sociologists at Work*. Basic Books, New York.

Haralambos, M. and Holborn, M. (1990) *Sociology: Themes and Perspectives*. 3rd edn. Unwin Hyman, London.

Hart, N. (1976) *When Marriage Ends*. Tavistock, London.

Hart, N. (1985) *The Sociology of Health and Medicine*. Causeway, Ormskirk.

Henry, I. C. and Pashley, G. (1990) *Health Care Research*. Health and Nursing Studies for Diploma and Undergraduate Students. Quay Publishing, Lancaster.

Hockey, L. (ed.) (1983) *Primary Care Nursing*. Churchill Livingstone, London.

Holmes, T. and Masuda, M. (1974) 'Life Changes in Illness Susceptibility'. In *Stressful Life Events: Their Nature and Effects*, ed. B. S. Dohren Wend. Wiley, New York.

Hughes, D. (1988) 'When Nurse Knows Best: Some Aspects of Nurses/Doctor Interaction in a Casualty Department'. *Sociology of Health and Illness*, 10 (1), 1–22.

Hunter, D. (1990) 'Organizing and Managing Health Care: A Challenge for Medical Sociology'. In S. Cunningham-Burley and N. McKeganey (eds), *Readings in Medical Sociology*. Tavistock/Routledge, London.

Hunter, D. and Judge, K. (1988) *Griffiths and Community Care: Meeting the Challenge*. King's Fund Institute, London.

Illich, I. (1977) *Disabling Professions*. Marion Boyars, London.

Inglis, B. (1981) *The Diseases of Civilisation*. Hodder & Stoughton, London.

Irvine, D. (1990) *Managing for Quality in General Practice*. King's Fund Centre for Health Services Development, London.

Jones, K., Brown, J. and Bradshaw, J. (1983) *Issues in Social Policy*. Rev. edn. Routledge & Kegan Paul, London.

Joseph, M. (1990) *Sociology for Everyone*. Polity Press, Cambridge.

Jowell, R., Witherspoon, S. and Brook, L. (eds) (1988) *British Social Attitudes – the 5th Report*. Gower, Aldershot.

Kennedy, I. (1981) *The Unmasking of Medicine*. Allen & Unwin, London.

Klein, J. (1965) *Samples from English Culture*, vols I and II. Routledge & Kegan Paul, London.

Kornhauser, A. (1965) *Mental Health and the Industrial Worker*. Wiley, New York.

Laing, R. D. (1960) *The Divided Self*. Tavistock, London.

Laing, R. D. (1967) *The Politics of Experience*. Penguin, Harmondsworth.

Laing, R. D. (1970) *Sanity, Madness and the Family*. Tavistock, London.

Laing, R. D. (1971a) *Knots*. Penguin, Harmondsworth.

Laing, R. D. (1971b) *Self and Others*. Penguin, Harmondsworth.

Lonsdale, S. (1982) *Women and Disability*. Macmillan, London.

Lonsdale, S. (1990) 'Grin and Bear It'. *Health Service Journal*, 100, 1822.

McGlew, T., Gilloran, A., McKee, K. and Robertson, A. (1988) *Staff Morale in Long-Stay Psychogeriatric Units*. Nursing Studies Association, University of Edinburgh.

Mackay, L. (1989) *Nursing a Problem*. Open University Press, Milton Keynes.

McNeill, P. (1985) *Research Methods*. Tavistock, London.

Mann, M. (ed.) (1983) *The Macmillan Student Encyclopaedia of Sociology*. Macmillan, London.

Mann, P. H. (1976) *Methods of Sociological Enquiry*. Blackwell, Oxford.

Mannheim, K. (1991) *Ideology and Utopia: An Introduction to the Sociology of Knowledge*. Routledge, London.

Marmot, M. G. (1987) 'Look After Your Heart'. *Health Trends*, 19, 21–5.

Marmot, M., Adelstein, A. and Bulusu, L. (1984) *Infant Mortality in England and Wales 1970–1978*. OPCS Studies on Medical and Population Issues, no. 47. HMSO, London.

Marmot, M. G. and McDowall, M. E. (1986) 'Mortality Decline and Widening Social Inequalities'. *Lancet*, 2 (8501), 274–6.

Marshall, G. (1990) *In Praise of Sociology*. Unwin Hyman, London.

Marshall, T. (1963) *Sociology at the Crossroads*. Heinemann, London.

Maxwell, R. (ed.) (1988) *Reshaping the National Health Service*. Policy Journals, Hermitage, Berkshire.

Merton, R. K. (1968) *Social Theory and Social Structure*. Free Press, New York.

Merton, R. K. et al. (1957) *The Student Physician*. Harvard University Press, Cambridge, Mass.

Miles, A. (1991) *Women, Health and Medicine*. Open University Press, Milton Keynes.

Mills, C. Wright (1970) *The Sociological Imagination*. Penguin, Harmondsworth.

Mini Dictionary for Nurses (1991). Oxford University Press.

Mitchell, J. (1984) *What is to be Done About Illness and Health?* Penguin, Harmondsworth.

Morgan, M., Calnan, M. and Manning, N. (1985) *Sociological Approaches to Health and Medicine*. Croom Helm, London.

Newson, J. and E. (1965) *Patterns of Infant Care in an Urban Community*. Penguin, Harmondsworth.

Newson, J. and E. (1970) *Four Years Old in an Urban Community*. Penguin, Harmondsworth.

Oakley, A. (1976) *Housewife*. Penguin, Harmondsworth.

Oakley, A. (1979a) *Becoming a Mother*. Martin Robertson, Oxford.

Oakley, A. (1979b) *From Here to Maternity*. Martin Robertson, Oxford.

Oakley, A. (1980) *Women Confined*. Martin Robertson, Oxford.

Oakley, A. (1982) *Subject Women*. Fontana, London.

Olesen, V. L. and Whittaker, E. W. (1968) *The Silent Dialogue*. Jossey-Bass, San Francisco.

Owen, P. and Glennerster, H. (1990) *Nursing in Conflict*. Macmillan, London.

Parkes, C., Benjamin, B. and Fitzgerald, R. (1969) 'Broken Heart: A Statistical Survey of Increased Mortality Among Widowers'. *British Medical Journal*, 4, 13–16.

Parsons, T. (1951) *The Social System*. Free Press, Glencoe.

Patrick, D. L. and Scambler, G. (eds) (1986) *Sociology as Applied to Medicine*. 2nd edn. Baillière Tindall, London.

Pearson, A. (ed.) (1988) *Primary Nursing*. Croom Helm, London.

Perkins, H. (1990) *The Rise of Professional Society: England since 1880*. Routledge, London.

Platt, S. and Kreitman, N. (1984) 'Trends in Parasuicide and Unemployment among Men in Edinburgh, 1968–1982'. *British Medical Journal*, 289 (6451), 1029–32.

Project 2000, Project Papers 1–9. United Kingdom Central Council for Nursing, Midwifery and Health Visiting, London.

Pugh, D. S. et al. (1983) *Writers on Organizations*. Penguin, Harmondsworth.

Radical Statistics Health Group (1987) *Facing the Figures: What Really is Happening in the National Health Service*. Radical Statistics, London.

Reid, I. (1989) *Social Class Differences in Britain*. 3rd edn. Fontana, London.

Roberts, H. (1985) *Patient/Patient: Women and their Doctors*. Pandora Press, London.

Rose, G. and Marmot, M. G. (1981) 'Social Class and Coronary Heart Disease'. *British Heart Journal*, 45, 13–19.

Roth, J. (1963) *Timetables*. Bobbs Merrill, Indianapolis.

Salvage, J. (1985) *The Politics of Nursing*. Heinemann Medical Books, London.

Scambler, G. (ed.) (1991) *Sociology as Applied to Medicine*. Baillière Tindall, London.

Schon, D. (1983) *The Reflective Practitioner*. Temple Smith, London.

Segalman, R. and Marsland, D. (1989) *From Cradle to Grave*. Macmillan, Basingstoke.

Silverman, D. (1987) *Communication and Medical Practice*. Sage, London.

Simpson, I. H. (1979) *From Student to Nurse*. American Sociological Association, USA.

Smith, G. J., Makinson, D. H. and Farrow, S. C. (1986) 'Learning to Swim with the Griffiths Tide', *British Medical Journal*, 292 (6513), 150–1.

Smith, P. (1992) *The Emotional Labour of Nursing*. Macmillan, London.

Stark, E. (1990) 'Rethinking Homicide: Violence, Race and the Politics of Gender'. *International Journal of Health Services*, 20 (1).

Strong, P. and Robinson, J. (1988) *New Model Management: Griffiths and the NHS*. Nursing Policy Studies Centre, Warwick.

Szasz, T. (1971) *The Manufacture of Madness*. Routledge & Kegan Paul, London.

Taylor, F. W. (1911) *The Principles of Scientific Management*. Harper, New York.

Thomas, K. W. (1976) 'Conflict and Conflict Management'. In M. Dunnette (ed.), *Handbook of Industrial and Organizational Psychology*, Rand McNally, Chicago.

Thompson, I. E., Melia, K. M. and Boyd, M. B. (1988) *Nursing Ethics*. Churchill Livingstone, London.

Thornes, B. and Collard, J. (1979) *Who Divorces?* Routledge & Kegan Paul, London.

Timio, M. and Gentili, S. (1976) 'Adrenosympathetic Overactivity during Conditions of Work Stress'. *British Journal of Preventative and Social Medicine*, 30 (4), 262–5.

Titmuss, R. (1968) *Commitment to Welfare*. Allen & Unwin, London.

Titmuss, R. (1976) *Essays on 'The Welfare State'*. 3rd edn. Allen & Unwin, London.

Townsend, P. and Davidson, N. (eds) (1982) *Inequalities in Health: The Black Report*. Penguin, Harmondsworth.

Townsend, P. and Davidson, N. (eds) (1988) *Inequalities in Health*. (Includes *The Black Report*; and Margaret Whitehead, *The Health Divide*.) Penguin, London.

Tuckett, M. (ed.) (1976) *An Introduction to Medical Sociology*. Tavistock, London.

Turner, B. S. (1987) *Medical Power and Social Knowledge*. Sage, London.

Tyler, A. (1992) 'Political Cripples'. *New Statesman & Society*, 5 (206), 21–2.

Vaughan, J. A. (1990) 'Student Nurse Attitudes to Teaching/Learning Methods'. *Journal of Advanced Nursing*, 15, 925–33.

Waine, C. (1992) 'First Division United'. *Health Service Journal*, 12 March.

Waissman, R. (1990) 'An Analysis of Doctor–Parent Interactions in the Case of Pediatric Renal Failure: The Choice of Home Dialysis'. *Sociology of Health and Illness*, 12 (4), 432–51.

Waitzkin, H. and Stoekle, J. (1972) 'The Communication of Information about Illness'. *Advances in Psychosomatic Medicine*, 8, 180–215.

Walker, B. and Waddington, I. (1991) 'AIDS and the Doctor–Patient Relationship'. *Social Studies Review*, 6 (4).

Walsh, M. and Ford, P. (1986) 'Rituals in Nursing: We Always Do It This Way'. *Nursing Times*, 85 (41), 26–35.

Weir, D. et al. (1988) *Community Medicine*. Heinemann, London.

White, A. (ed.) (1989) *Health in the Inner City*. Heinemann, London.

Whitehead, M. (1988) *The Health Divide*. Penguin, London.

Wilmott, P. and Young, M. (1971) *Family and Class in a London Suburb*. Mentor, London.

Wilson, A. (1991) 'Start Up and Nurse Socialization'. *Journal of Advanced Nursing*, 16, 1478–86.

Worsley, P. (1987) *The New Introductory Sociology*. 3rd edn. Penguin, Harmondsworth.

Wright, S. G. (1986) *Building and Using a Model of Nursing*. Arnold, London.

Wright, S. G. (1990) *Changing Nursing Practice*. Arnold, London.

Young, M. and Willmott, P. (1957) *Family and Kinship in East London*. Routledge & Kegan Paul, London.

Zola, I. K. (1973) 'Pathways to the Doctor: From Person to Patient'. *Social Science and Medicine*, 7, 677–89.

Journals

Ageing and Society
Behavioural Neuroscience
British Journal of Psychology
British Medical Bulletin
British Medical Journal
The Carer
Child Poverty Action Group
Counselling
Health Trends
Health Visitor
Journal of Access Studies
Journal of Advanced Nursing
Journal of Applied Psychology
Journal of Organizational Behaviour
Journal of Research in Personality
New Age Concern
Nursing Times

Practical Caring
Social Forces
Social History of Medicine
Social Science and Medicine
Social Work Today
Sociology of Health and Illness
Wild Health

Index